Jacinda Ardern

Biography

The Journey of an Extraordinary Prime Minister

Antonio Smith

CHAPTER 1

After driving for 30 miles in the Kāingaroa Forest, one may wonder if there is anything left on earth other than trees. That's the view: radiata trees, each 100 feet tall, in neat gridlines that stretch as far as the eye can see. The forest is both large and dense, with trees, rows, and miles upon miles. The monotony is broken only by two things. The road first carved through the murky countryside, followed by the radiata shoots, which appeared randomly and stubbornly. These tiny, wilding pines resemble the Christmas trees of my childhood—joyful yet sad, with only a few scant branches, enough for a single thread of tinsel that will never completely conceal the exposed trunk.

The first time I visited Murupara, I was four years old and sick with the flu in the backseat of my family's beige 1979 Toyota Corona. In those days, I was also prone to vehicle sickness, which was very certainly exacerbated by my corduroy booster seat, which was essentially a wedge of solid foam wrapped in fabric. It increased my height, but it also emphasized every turn in the road. My sister Louise, who is only eighteen months older than me, sat beside me. She was also in a booster. She was nervous, but not enough to stop asking my parents things like, "How much longer?" Why can't we stop? What if I need to use the toilet? We all held our plush bears, which we remarkably resembled. Teddy, my dog, had a round friendly face, a squat frame, and short legs. My sister's bear, Cookie, was nearly twice as long as mine, with a slim torso and lengthy legs.

The windows were rolled down just enough for me to hang my fingers over the top and wriggle them in the fresh air. Beneath my hanging feet were the materials that my mother made sure were with us on every long car trip: an old towel and an empty, half-gallon plastic ice cream container in case we had to puke up. She never threw anything away, and this container would most certainly be repurposed to keep homemade blueberry muffins. Between me and Louise, locked within a cardboard box with little openings at the top, was the most unpleasant passenger of all: our gray rescue cat, Norm. The sedation from the vet was wearing off as he rubbed his face against the top of the box, whiskers poking through the perforations.

It was a moving day. We had left behind friends and relatives in Hamilton, more than two hours to the northwest, since my father got a new job as a police sergeant in Murupara, a place I'd never been.

Throughout my childhood, he ran 10,000 kilometers. When he got home, he'd replace his running shoes with worn-out sheepskin slippers and sit in his La-Z-Boy chair to read the newspaper. Dad is happiest when he is reading, especially about world history, Antarctic expedition, and the legendary explorer Ernest Shackleton.

Most of all, Dad was interested in people and wanted to know about their lives. As a police officer, he wanted to know not only what crimes had been committed, but also why. I'd frequently hear him comment that the police can't arrest their way out of everything. He felt that to solve crime, you needed to understand why it was happening in the first place. He asked wonderful questions, and people spoke to him. It wasn't uncommon for someone my father was questioning to pause and say, "At least you're listening to me." That's not to suggest he was soft. I doubt anyone could say that about my father, who investigated homicides, rapes, robberies, and gang activity. He simply approached challenges from a new perspective.

When Dad finished his exam that day, he found a message waiting for him: come to the hospital. He arrived in time to welcome me into the world.

Dad enjoyed his work in Hamilton and became a detective constable, but he aspired to lead a station rather than simply working at one. So, when I was a toddler, he started studying for his sergeant's exams, which was no easy task. He already had a full-time career, a young family, and was quite involved in the Mormon religion. To prepare, he got up before dawn and studied for an hour or two before the rest of us awoke. He would study again after nightfall.

The forest around Murupara felt towering, but the small town itself was low and open, with flat, utilitarian houses.

Despite being named after trees (Kauri, Rimu, Pūriri), the streets lacked trees. It was a forestry town that did not have its own forest.

Our new home was on Kōwhai Avenue, named for a small, woody tree with vivid yellow flowers in the spring. The house was a compact rectangle of cream brick, simple and functional, with a little corrugated-iron garage on one side. There was no garden, only a concrete road leading to the front door. But nearly as soon as the moving trucks came, my mother began preparing our new home, hanging draperies and planting pansies in the yard.

What our new house lacked in size, it made up for with a massive, open backyard. The yard was spacious enough to accommodate a trampoline and a rotary clothesline, which my sister and I circled while learning to ride our bikes. If Louise and I jumped high enough on the trampoline, we could see the blue roof of the police station fade in and out of sight.

Hamish, my father's coworker and police constable, lived next door to us with his wife, Joan. Except for her friendliness, I don't remember much about Joan. Hamish was around the same age as my father, lean, with a thinning crop of golden hair. There was only one other officer stationed at the station, and he, Hamish, and my father comprised the entire Murupara Police Force. These three officers patrolled not only Murupara but also the vast, rural, and isolated surrounding districts. Backup reinforcements were nearly an hour distant.

In 1984, a new government led by Labour Party leader David Lange was elected, and the minister of finance, Roger Douglas, implemented changes that transformed New Zealand's economy, which had previously been among the most controlled and protected in the world, into one of the most open. Parts of the economy previously owned by the state, particularly forestry, were privatized and gutted in a method known as Rogernomics.

Murupara's transformations were harsh. In the years before our arrival, more than half of the town's forestry workers had lost their jobs. Many people who were able to depart did so. Businesses closed, and many people sank deeper into poverty.

This was hardly the first blow to the small community. Māori, who formed up the majority of the settlement, were already bearing the ravages of colonization. Abel Tasman, a Dutch explorer, first saw what is now known as Aotearoa, New Zealand—the land of the long white cloud—in 1642. Then came James Cook, followed by whalers, traders, Christian missionaries, and pioneers. These waves of arrivals frequently had severe consequences for tangata whenua, the inhabitants of the land, including land seizure, battle, loss of life, wealth, and mana—dignity. Rogernomics exacerbated this history.

Murupara was where I initially attended school. I wasn't quite five years old, but the school indicated that there was little purpose in waiting for my birthday, and that I should start kindergarten as Louise did in second grade. We began strolling together on a cold winter day. That first morning, the teacher announced the roll alphabetically. My surname placed me at the top of the list, and when my name was called, I sat up on the mat, legs crossed in front of me, and cried, "Yes!" " returned warmly. As the teacher called the roll, some students responded with "Āe," which means "yes" in Māori. All I did was notice it. I grew up with Māori vocabulary used interchangeably with English, such as "stomach," "family," "European," and "love" being regularly replaced with puku, whānau, pākehā and aroha.

My family had Māori relations on both sides, and we were Mormons. In New Zealand, Māori were a significant portion of the Mormon church membership. This was the first time I was surrounded by youngsters speaking te reo Māori openly.

Today, I am aware that I was on the territory of the Ngāti Manawa people, a local Māori tribe. In previous decades, continuous fighting on their land resulted in crop loss, the Crown breached leasing agreements, and sickness destroyed their population.

I had no idea when I was five. I just saw the phrases the same way I noticed other things. The school grounds were massive, huge enough for extensive games of tag. We had mat time and stories. That on Fridays, we could have fish and chips, which came in tightly wrapped newspaper that we ripped open to delve into the sizzling dish. That other youngsters, like myself, enjoyed going barefoot in the summer—sometimes even to school.

Not long after starting school, Louise and I were heading home when we heard crying. It was a younger boyr than I was. He was just across the street, with his back to us. He was alone. It was cold by now, the type of cold that caused snow to fall on mountain ranges and ice to form on puddle tops. It was the kind of cold that seeped into your bones, but this boy was wearing shorts and his feet were bare. He had a massive bag that dwarfed him totally. Brown streaks, resembling feces, flowed down the backs of his legs.

My sister and I slowed down. The boy sobbed loudly, sounding like he was suffocating. I was still very young, yet I was mature enough to have a persistent thought. He should not be alone. My sister and I clasped hands and silently observed him. I suppose we both agreed that it was best if he didn't know we had seen him. We watched him go away from us, and all the while I silently pleaded, "Please." Please come and find him.

When our family needed groceries, we'd get into the Toyota Corona and drive an hour to the Pak 'n Save in Rotorua. We'd return through the deep, dark forest, till the fragrance of pine gave way to the sulfuric smell of Rotorua's hot springs. One Saturday, my car sickness got the best of me, and I vomited on my clothes. The rest of the drive was spent with the windows down, as my mother lamented not bringing an ice cream container. When we got in Rotorua, my father drove me to the police station, where he literally hosed me off while my mother picked up a brand-new suit. I recall it clearly: a pale green floral skirt with embroidered trim and a matching shirt with a round collar. It was one of the few dresses I owned back then that wasn't hand-me-down or hand-sewn. After that bonus outfit, I dreaded vehicle sickness a little less.

Despite the long travel, Louise and I enjoyed our Saturday trips to Rotorua, especially in the beginning when we didn't have many friends. The other students at school were understandably wary of us. We weren't just the new kids or the outsiders; we were the daughters of the police sergeant, who locked people up. Louise faced suspicion. She was called names and teased, so I started following Louise about during lunchtime like a self-appointed protector.

Perhaps this is why Dad wanted to start his own station in the first place. Since becoming a police officer, he'd witnessed numerous instances in which a parent would reach down to a youngster and mumble a warning of some kind. Do you see the policeman there? If you're naughty, he'll come and arrest you. Dad would tell me how much he despised it when children were told that. He wanted people to believe their lives had improved because the cops were around. However, that type of policing requires trust, which takes time.

One day, I went into town, cutting across the backyard to the police station parking lot. There, I noticed a gathering of men in leather pants and coats gathered around a figure in blue uniform: my father. He was shorter than the men around him, and he was alone. The men moved around him slowly and menacingly, kicking up loose gravel as they went. Even from a distance, I could feel Dad's body tense; he kept one arm out in front of himself, as if trying to keep the men quiet while also keeping them at a distance. Even though I was too tiny to comprehend everything that was going on, I felt the situation was bad. Several months into our stay, a brawl broke out on the lawn between our house and Hamish's. As my mother observed from the kitchen window, around twenty men emerged from a nearby party, intoxicated and swearing, throwing filthy fists at one another. Brawls like these were not uncommon, and they typically ended fast. But this one kept going. When the men turned away from each other, they became acutely aware of their surroundings.

"Let us smash the sergeant's windows!" " One of them shouted.

The windows nearest them were the same ones where my sister and I slept. My mother did a quick calculation. Should she wake us up and move us or let us sleep? She resolved to spare Louise and me the stress of a late-night wake-up by turning to the best safeguard she could think of: prayer.

My mother grew up a Presbyterian, the daughter of conservative farmers on a 144-acre dairy farm in rural Waikato, where the nearest little town was five miles away. She was one of five children; it would have been seven, but my grandmother lost twin boys soon after they were born, a loss she attributed to the difficulties of farm life and the fact that she milked cows until their birth.

Dad rode a motorcycle, had long hair in the back, and wore flared pants and plaid shirts. But he opened the car door for my mother, and being a Mormon, he didn't drink, which relieved her. Dad never attempted to convert my mother. However, when they began dating, Mum went on a vacation to the Gold Coast of Australia, where she met Mormon missionaries and read the Book of Mormon for the first time. Something clicked. She enjoyed the ideology, the members' direct and personal contact with God, and the emphasis on service and concern for others. For her, it felt real. She did not need her parents' permission to convert, and she did not acquire it. My grandparents were Baptists, and they didn't consider Mormonism a legitimate faith. Despite her parents' misgivings, my mother was baptized and married in a Mormon church.

Which is how she ended up praying while a drunken crowd contemplating shattering the windows beneath which her daughters slept. Whether it was divine intervention or simply good police training, my father and Hamish arrived and eventually dispersed the crowds, leaving our windows intact. Soon after, the cops built a fence in front of our home.

My mother was still wary about disturbing my father. Extremely careful. One night, I found my father's shackles and managed to lock myself within. My mom couldn't find the key anywhere in the home. So, even though Dad was only next door at the station, I sat there with those heavy cuffs around my wrists, learning a lesson until he got home.

All this activity was taxing for Mum. When we relocated to Murupara, she was only 29 years old and already had two young children to care for. Her family was far away, and Dad was usually working. Even her compensated employment did not provide much of a break. When Dad returned home, she would go to the police station and clean it on her own, earning $4.18 per hour.

Meanwhile, Louise struggled in school. She was tall for her age, but she was also leaner and skinnier than I was. One day, I was home sick when Louise, who was just six, arrived at the end of the day crying. She informed my mother that a gang of boys had pinned her down and sat on her, striking her on the head and body.

Mum was aware that Louise was having difficulty establishing friends and that children occasionally mistreated us. But, until that afternoon, Mom had no idea I'd been following my sister around the playground, or that things were so bad that Louise could be physically wounded. This was too much for her.

My mother brought us to a neighboring school eight miles outside of town and requested that we enroll. The principal refused. My mother waited a week before returning and asking again. Maybe the principal had a change of heart. Perhaps he anticipated my mother would persevere until he consented. So he conceded. After that, every morning at 7:45 a.m., Louise and I boarded a school bus in front of the Murupara Hotel for the thirty-minute ride to school in Galatea.

My mother's diary from the early days of Murupara contains a matter-of-fact entry. Dad had been sent to make an arrest in a nearby town, and he returned with his uniform damaged. When Mum questioned what had happened, his response was noticeably brief. She deduced from his silence that he had been assaulted during the arrest. This diary entry is unusual for its lack of emotion. Mum was simply conveying facts.

However, Mum soon reports having difficulty breathing. Reading these pages today, it's evident to me that she had begun to experience panic attacks. However, this was the 1980s, long before terms like "panic attack" became prevalent. Even then, there were no lengthy descriptions or laments about how difficult she finds things. Just wanted to mention that she had moments when she couldn't breathe. Mum stayed stoic and cheerful. That is, until she couldn't.

For the most part, I don't remember my mother struggling. She fought hard to keep it from us. Her diary recounts that when we drove back toward Murupara after getting groceries, there was a turnoff where she would always start crying silently. However, she was determined that my sister and I would not see her.

On one occasion, however, I did notice. Mum and I were home alone. I walked into the kitchen and saw my mother leaning against the kitchen counter. She didn't turn toward me like she always did, and she didn't inquire what I needed in the same manner my mother did for everyone she loved and cared about. Mom didn't seem to notice I was there. She wasn't pottering, fussing, baking scones, or cooking lunch.

Her back was to me, apron strings wrapped around her midsection. Both hands were pressed against the edge of the stainless-steel counter, with one clutching a tea towel so tightly that it appeared to be offering her something in exchange for her might. She rocked back and forth just slightly. I didn't have to see her face to know she was crying.

I wanted her to know that I was present. I hoped that would break her of whatever was causing her sadness. I came up beside her leg. But as I approached her, she spun on her heels and walked to the back door. She disappeared through the doorway, holding the tea cloth.

I looked after her. Then I followed, half-running to catch up. But my tiny legs could not keep up with her stride. As I watched her go away from me, I felt bewilderment and panic rise in my chest. I wanted to know if she was okay. I also did not want to be alone. I was too small to be alone.

Mum walked across the yard to the gate that connected our property to Hamish's. Then she disappeared a second time. When I got to Hamish's back door and entered the kitchen, my mother was seated at the table, head bowed over her tea towel. Joan, Hamish's wife, was next to her. When I recall this event today, I can't see Joan's face. I remember her as a presence, with her legs next to Mum and one hand on Mum's shoulder. Joan was always sympathetic to me and Louise.

But when she turned away from Mum and toward me, she appeared concentrated and serious.

"Go home, Jacinda," she instructed. Her voice was crisp and forceful. But my home is here, I reasoned. My mother is here.

CHAPTER 2

I don't recall the days following my mother's collapse. I know my mom was home with us, but she claims to have spent the majority of that time sleeping. Nobody explained much. I'm not sure how to effectively describe a nervous breakdown to a toddler. But I now understand what happened.

I also acknowledge that my father did everything he could to help. He would come home from his job and prepare meals, iron, and assist us clean our room. He took us all to the beach on Mount Maunganui for a break, which reportedly helped.

However, when we returned, Mum's silent tears at the Rainbow Mountain turnoff to Murupara reappeared. Following the trip, my mother noted in her diary that she was feeling "unwell again." The next morning, she woke up long enough to get my sister and me to school before crawling back into bed.

In the end, I believe three things helped Mum persevere: her religion, her church community, and trout fishing.

There are various rivers near Murupara, and Mum decided at some point that she would educate herself how to catch trout. The activity served as both a mini-vacation and possibly a means of regaining some control over life. She'd get her pole, unwillingly put me and Louise into the car, and drive off into the middle of nowhere. I can still imagine her: standing on the edge of the flowing water in her large spectacles, bright green gym shorts with white piping at the borders, and a tight pocket tee over top. She would stand there for hours, completely concentrated. Meanwhile, Louise and I sat on the riverbank, very bored. We played with sticks and invented imaginary games until we couldn't take it anymore.

"Muuuuum…," we would complain. "Can we go home?"

Mum would softly cast again.

"Mummmm, we need to go to the toilet!"

Keeping her gaze fixed on the lake, she'd reply impatiently, "Well, go find a tree." That was ultimately what we would do.

People occasionally offered to assist her fish. She might take the occasional class or their recommendations for new places to try. But I believe Mum preferred to be out there alone, doggedly learning this new ability. I saw Mum cast several times. But I only remember one fish being caught. It wasn't very enormous, but it was plenty for Dad to smoke it in the garden and for us all to tell Mum how tasty her hard-earned catch was.

Every Sunday, we met in that classroom for three hours of services. We spent the first hour together for sacrament and a few lectures. For my parents, small-town services meant being ready to get up and make a lecture at any time in case the member appointed to be a speaker did not show up. Then Louise and I would walk off to have lessons and activities while the grownups went to Sunday school. Then we would split up into two groups: Relief Society for the ladies and Priesthood meetings for the men.

We got to know a few other church members, and Mum went out of her way to help everyone who needed it. There was the couple that had recently purchased a house when they separated. Mum assisted them in getting their affairs in order, particularly the wife, who had recently become a single mother with two children and one on the way. Mum paid her several visits, using her bookkeeping abilities and assisting her with budgeting and other tasks. When the baby arrived, Mum paid her a visit at the maternity hospital. I recall watching from the doorway as Mum wrapped her arms around this woman, her face beaming. They were, as I now realize, two women who needed each other.

Walter occasionally brought over his collection of cards. While most kids our age liked to collect wrestling cards, Walter collected the cards that came with trial perfume bottles, each flavored with a spritz of fragrance. Walter placed the cards into an old school workbook, and we'd go through them together, Walter pointing out his favorites or pretending we were working at a pharmacy. I'd lift the book to my face, attempting to detect any lingering aroma of wildflowers or vanilla. I often smelled nothing at all. But I pretended that I did. What mattered more than the aroma was Walter's expression of genuine excitement as we poured over these wonderful cards.

This strategy did not always yield the same results. My father traveled to Ruatāhuna, a little settlement of only a few hundred people, to speak with someone who had been growing enormous cannabis crops. It was an hour's drive back to the Murupara station, so my father invited the man to visit the next time he was in town.

Instead, the man decided to "go bush," and set off for a home deep in the jungle. His sudden transfer was not a secret, but he used his remote position as a barrier. My father is compassionate but tough. If you do not follow through, he will. On my mother's thirty-first birthday, Dad got up at 6:00 a.m., grabbed his backpack, and went out the door. He hiked for four hours on the outskirts of Ruatāhuna, crossing a large river eight times before reaching the man's hut.

The man greeted him with a disappointed expression. "I've been worried about you showing up," he added with a sigh.

About a year into our stint in Murupara, my father volunteered for the dunk tank at the local school fair. The weather was cold, as seen by the numerous sweatshirts and jackets seen in images from that day. One of the photographs has Dad perched on a perilous wooden plank above a tank of frigid water. His feet are naked, although he is otherwise dressed in full costume. He's smiling gamely, hands on his thighs, but his fingers are spread wide, as if he's waiting for the moment when someone hits the target with a ball, releasing him into the water underneath. Surrounding him are local residents—children, parents, and teachers—all eager to take their turn throwing the police chief into the water.

Dad is wet in the next snap, clearly recovering from one of his many plunges. Around him, people are laughing. My mother isn't in the picture, but I know she was there, just out of shot, smiling at Dad and holding a dry towel and a spare pair of clothes.

After nearly three years in the modest square house behind the police station, my family packed up the Toyota Corona again as a large truck reversed into our front yard to pick up the Crown Lynn dining set and our scratchy wooden couch in January 1988. By this point, I'd lived nearly half my life in Murupara, but Dad got a new job.

In the future, when people ask me where I'm from, Murupara will not be my response. However, two decades later, as a newly elected MP sitting in my office, a journalist asked me a different question. Our two chairs were facing each other, with a notepad placed on the journalist's lap and one arm outstretched to hold a Dictaphone.

"So," she inquired, "when did you first become political?"

I tapped my fingers over my lap, staring first at her, then at the tape. Behind her sat a tall wooden bookcase filled with blue-bound copies of laws. My workstation, which featured a green leather inlay and a tall reclining chair, overlooked the parliamentary atrium.

For a brief period, I looked at the bright light from the lamp in the corner and imagined myself in a completely different location. I envisioned a row of residences with large open streets. I noticed the sun bouncing off the black carpet of a trampoline, bare feet skipping over sidewalk cracks, and piles of twenty-cent lollipops. I noticed a small-framed boy clutching his book of scent cards, and another dwarfed by his backpack, strolling and crying alone. I considered justice and how circumstances might push a community into difficulty—and how the inhabitants in that community were able to retain their mana and dignity. I thought of my parents—my father, who was doing his best to help rather than hurt, and my mother, who was also doing her best. And I knew the answer: Murupara.

I became politically involved since I lived in Murupara.

CHAPTER 3

I have a specific facial feature that is not commonly called a big smile. If you stood on my left side, you would notice a thin white scar that starts at the inner corner of my eye and runs diagonally down the seam of my nose to the outer edge of my nostril. The scar is a persistent reminder of my nearly continual need to be "useful." It is also a physical recall of the little, three-acre orchard on the outskirts of Morrinsville, the dairy farming community I will always call home.

I first learned about the orchard when my mother's parents, Granddad Eric and Grandma Margaret, owned it. The orchard was my grandparents' second try at a fresh venture after selling their dairy farm, which they had owned and worked for thirty years.

My grandfather Eric, a towering guy with keen features, was equally impatient and intense. Eric was always working on a project, whether it was fixing, harvesting, experimenting, or enhancing. He was usually dressed in his distinctive woolen shorts and knee-high socks. He was a man with a constant, unwavering mission. When we went to the orchard, I would occasionally look into the garage and see him talk to himself while working, as my mother always did. He might say to himself as he moves through tasks. Place this here, followed by this. He would occasionally hum or sing a tune. Either would add a rare lightness to his otherwise austere face.

Dad once informed me that Granddad Eric was the smartest person he had ever met. Everywhere I looked in that orchard, there was proof of Granddad's ingenuity—the patched-up apple grader, the bright red tractor he'd rebuilt, and old images of boats he'd constructed himself. He'd built entire houses before, but this one—a creaking, two-story timber-framed "Lockwood," a design distinguished by exposed timber walls and interconnecting beams—he'd renovated and completed.

Granddad's busy schedule meant he had little patience for mistakes, even from small children. So Louise and I "helped" Grandma instead. I can't recall ever seeing Grandma Margaret in anything other than a long skirt and blouse, her hair styled like Queen Elizabeth, but with a touch of Julia Child mayhem.

Sometimes mother loaded me and Louise into a trailer my grandfather had built, linked to a riding lawn mower, and drove us about the orchard. We sat there on hard wood, bumping and lurching next to trays of fruits, staring at the back of Grandma Margaret's head while her corgi trotted behind us. My grandmother may have chosen the breed as an homage to the queen, but she was far from fancy or regal. Perhaps this is why her dog was just named Shannon.

Every now and then, Grandma Margaret looked around to make sure we weren't leaning too close to the trailer's edge, flashing a smile of perfectly white artificial teeth before returning her eyes to the sandy driveway. She was eager to chuckle and flung her head back. During those enormous belly laughs, her false teeth would occasionally fall out of her gums, reminding me of the chewy teeth we used to get in the lollipop mix at the corner store.

When Granddad Eric sold the family dairy farm, he transitioned to kiwifruit, then nashi pears. By 1988, just as we were leaving Murupara, he had set his sights on the next big thing: avocados in Tauranga. My father got a new job, a promotion to detective sergeant in neighboring Hamilton. My folks were looking for a house, and Granddad wanted to sell.

My grandparents sold the orchard to my parents for more pragmatic than sentimental reasons. My parents took out a mortgage and a loan from my grandparents at 18 percent interest, which was about the going rate at the time. Purchasing the orchard was a costly and risky decision for my parents. For me, the orchard seemed both a homecoming and a magnificent journey.

Our two-story house was substantially larger than the one we had in Murupara, with enough space for Louise and me to each have our own bedroom. Our house was in the outskirts of town, next to a cornfield and the Morrinsville Golf Course. For the remainder of our time there, I heard periodic dull thuds on the roof or thwacks on the glass of windows, indicating that another inexperienced golfer had just teed off.

To the west lay a tiny woodland of about three acres. This land was sparse, with only a few pine trees and some undergrowth. But for me and Louise, it was a puzzle to be solved. In the forest, tree stumps transformed into fictional individuals with backstories, living a world unique to myself and Louise. We sometimes uncovered goodies in the forest, such as beer cans, snack wrappers, and even condoms. We once discovered a G-string, a thin strip of fabric peeping through the weeds, and dug it away. Mum taught me where babies come from when we were at Murupara. "I don't want you learning about it from some kid at school," she'd said, handing up a picture book full of images that made me want to shield my eyes. Still, I couldn't quite connect that book to the lace floss at the end of the stick.

When we weren't playing in the forest, Louise and I worked in the orchard. My parents had taken on a big responsibility by moving to a working orchard, and we were now old enough to help without being a complete nuisance. Dad spent his days solving crimes and arrests. Then, in the evening, he'd go through the door, change into shorts and an old shirt, put on his Red Band gumboots, which had worn the hair off his calf muscles, and go back outdoors. I'd sometimes hop on my bike and pedal following him, observing as he entered the shed, strapped the chemical sprayer to his back, and proceeded along the rows of trees, spraying pesticide.

My uncle Mark, Mum's younger brother, was involved in an accident in a neighboring city five months after we moved to Morrinsville. Mark shared my grandfather Eric's height, and his powerful jaw and nose. His hair was cut in a brown mullet, and while he'd occasionally assisted my grandparents in the orchard, he mostly worked in rural factories, just enough to keep his prized car running with its loud engine and shiny paint job. Mum went back and forth to the hospital, and I bombarded her with questions. Was he awake yet? Was he getting better? Could they test his brain to discover whether he was still there? Could they know for certain? I wanted to see him for myself, but I was also terrified. When Mum couldn't find someone to stay with us at home, she bundled me and Louise into her car and drove us to the hospital.

It was June, winter in New Zealand, and I could see my breath as we crossed the parking lot. However, everything within the hospital seemed stale and out of season. We followed Mum along seemingly endless corridors, catching glimpses of rolling metal carts and waiting rooms with people seated in vinyl seats. Finally, somewhere deep inside the hospital, Mum pushed open a swinging door, and we followed her into a room smelling of disinfectant and packed with beds separated by curtains. My grandparents emerged through one curtain, but I scarcely noticed them. My gaze was fixated on the hospital bed in front of me.

My towering, swaggering uncle now lay on his back, completely still. His complexion was pallid. Only a few strands of hair showed out from the bandages that around his head. His eyes appeared to be swollen shut. An accordion-like device rose and fell in sync with Uncle Mark's chest, and a plastic tube protruded from his throat. How could something so terrible, so suffocating, be allowing him to breathe? Behind him, equipment beeped, recording vital indications that I didn't comprehend.

I stood still, pretending I wasn't afraid of the equipment and tubes. The adults whispered among themselves before heading out into the hallway—perhaps to speak with a doctor, or to converse out of Mark's earshot, just in case. Louise and I were left alone with our uncle and all the machines.

Weeks passed, and my uncle remained unconscious. Mum's answers to my questions became sadder and less promising. With no signs of progress, the physicians became increasingly persuaded that Mark's brain had died; without the machines and apparatus, his body would almost certainly follow. My mother was at the hospital when my grandparents made the impossible decision to discontinue their only son's life support.

That night, once Mum arrived home, I listened to her tell my father what had happened. She had been looking through the small window into Mark's room as the medical experts began to turn off the equipment. The accordion that had previously allowed him to breathe stopped moving. Everyone expected his body to shut down too. Instead, my uncle started coughing and gasping for air. Mum watched as seconds passed, which she described as seeming like minutes or an eternity. Coughing gradually reduced, giving way to rasping. Then, finally, a beat.

He was breathing. My uncle, Mark, was still living.

Over the next few weeks, the depth of my uncle's injuries became apparent. He ultimately awoke, but he was legally blind and had sustained substantial brain damage. But they were all words. The reality was more than that. I observed my uncle attempt to eat and drink again, struggle to click the top of a ballpoint pen while lying in bed, and learn to walk. He would never again go without support or attention. For the time being, his family, including my mother, would provide that care.

Nana was a proud woman. She always maintained her mother came to New Zealand from Scotland with only three things: her son, a pistol, and a violin. I never knew much about my great-grandmother, but I imagined her to be like my nana: brave, hilarious, and little frightening.

Nana had a deep gray perm that she had set every Friday in town. The chemicals occasionally tinged her hair a faint shade of purple. Her house, located close to Te Aroha Domain, was not fancy, but it was always cleaned, polished, and vacuumed to within an inch of its life.

Nana spent most of her time in the kitchen. Food was her love language, and she sometimes used it forcibly. If there were road workmen on her street, Nana would bake scones and make tea, then go out to them and say, "Now, come and sit down for a minute, boys." Have something to eat. Come now! "

In her own home, in a small alcove near the back door, she kept a stack of baking tins that I believed were magical. They were packed with the most wonderful, buttery shortbread, and no matter how much Dad and I ate, they never seemed to run out.

Nana was nearly always wearing an apron tied around her waist, woolen slippers on her feet, and her favorite orange-and-white fluffy yappy puppy Dinky rushing around. "Get out of this, Dinky! " She frequently snapped as she went through the kitchen. Nana's wrath was occasionally directed at those she cared about the most.

But no one drew Nana's wrath more than what she called "blue-tongue Tories." Nana joined the Labour Party in 1938 and served as the local party's chair, conducting meetings in her front room. She believed in helping people who worked hard and had little, and she was not afraid to take on those who didn't. Apparently, anytime Robert Muldoon, New Zealand's conservative prime minister during my early years, came on television, she would stand up and snap it off before he said anything.

During those monthly Sunday visits, while Nana bustled around the kitchen and the rest of the family chattered, Granddad Harry sat quietly at the Formica table, leaning back against the wall, legs crossed, toying with a bottle cap or loose wire. He would periodically pause to look around or smooth what remained of his hair across the top of his head before continuing to fidget.

I understood the story behind the scars: When Marie was four years old, she discovered a box of matches in the shed where my grandmother washed clothes in an old copper bathtub. Her small fingers managed to ignite a match, and her polyester outfit caught fire. My grandfather's coworker, Jim, noticed her as she stumbled out of the burning washhouse. Jim dashed to Marie, pushing her to the ground and rolling her down the slope in an attempt to extinguish the flames.

Marie's body bore the ramifications of that moment for many years, with a scar left by Jim's hand on her side. While Jim most certainly saved her life, 80 percent of Marie's body was burned that day, and she would spend the remainder of her life undergoing surgery. Perhaps it is why Aunty Marie was so outgoing and brassy.

Louise disliked television, particularly the six o'clock news bulletin. "Isn't the purpose of a family supper to spend time together and talk? " Louise occasionally grumbled. "Don't sit around in silence with the TV on!" "

"Shh," Mum would say in response. "We are listening to the news! "

Mum, on the other hand, was not always able to remain mute. She wasn't outwardly political and didn't share her parents' conservative views. But she adhered to a worldview that valued fairness and common sense. Every now and then, she'd hear something on television that enraged her, and she'd lose her cool at the table. If she saw a high-profile court case with an unsatisfactory verdict, she may exclaim at the screen, "Who judges the judges? Who judges the judges? " Mum was always a patient, methodical eater, but in these instances, she'd wave her fork frantically. She once became so worked up that a maize kernel became lodged in her throat, requiring medical attention to remove—a fact my father never forgot to remind her of.

"Be careful, Laurell," Dad would say quietly. "You're going to end up back at the hospital."

"I'm just browned off," Mum would reply, shaking her head and placing her fork on the side of her plate. "Sometimes the people in charge just really brown me off."

For the most part, I observed quietly, trying to take everything in. I had never traveled abroad, taken an aircraft, or left New Zealand's North Island. But from my kitchen table, I watched the Lockerbie bombing and photos of the Berlin Wall collapsing as people celebrated in its ruins. I witnessed a lone protester stop tanks in Tiananmen Square and Nelson Mandela walk out of prison. These stories did not always make sense to me, but they had an impact. The community I lived in, the life I had, appeared so different from what I saw on the television every night. But it didn't. As long as there were individuals in the photographs, I felt a connection to them. They also showed me something. I understood how huge the world is and how delicate life can be. However, it is not so large that a single person cannot make an impact.

Whatever they didn't buy, we kept and stored in our own food store closet, which stretched from the floor to the roof of the garage. When my friends came over, they would catch glances of the rows and rows of jars and cans, and because none of them were Mormons, their eyes would widen slightly. "Whoooo!" they may exclaim. "How much food do you have in here, anyway!?" "Can we play shop?" Like 'real' shops?" "If the end of the world comes, I'm coming here!"

That's when I realized how confusing my family's religion was to certain people. I wasn't always sure how to convey it either. How do you explain something so personal? When I couldn't find an answer to a question or felt something was unjust or dangerous, I turned to religion. I enjoyed how prayer could be used to solve almost any problem. Did you lose something important? Pray. Do you feel sad, anxious, anxious? Pray. Does your stomach hurt? Pray. Sometimes I found myself in silent prayer without even realizing I was doing it. They usually opened with the same words: "Dear Heavenly Father." Then I told God everything I was glad for—my mother and father, my home, and, on occasion, my sister—because my mother taught me that asking for something without first being appreciative is inappropriate. Then I'd make my request, and if I was desperate, I'd add a plea bargain: "Help me find Teddy, and I promise to clean my room."

Church taught me not only ideals but also how to manage my time effectively. There were always many service opportunities. We scrubbed the headstones at the local cemetery, sung at the local old people's home, and cleaned the chapel from top to bottom, sweeping floors and sanitizing urinals while adding round cleaning balls that resembled Gobstoppers but smelled bad. We were always able to service something or someone.

The religion also helped me determine what I wanted to do when I grew up: get married. When I was little, I even informed my mother that I would need to save $100 for when I got married since it was "expensive." And I would have children. My future was set. Just as long as I

When I was eight, I was baptized into the Church of Jesus Christ of Latter-day Saints. Baptism, one of the church's thirteen articles of faith, not only recognizes formal membership, as it does in many faiths, but it also cleanses a person of sin.

Following my baptism, we held a small celebration with curried eggs, potato chips, and chocolate cake. While the adults spoke, my inquisitive younger cousin, who was only seven, bombarded me with so many questions that I struggled to keep up. I did my best to respond until she asked a question I didn't expect: "Do you know where babies come from?" I realized she needed to be told this by an adult, someone who had the unique picture book Mum had shown me. But she was relentless, and the more she asked, the more I hesitated, until I finally cracked.

I spent the following five years working and playing in the orchard after school and on weekends. Mum's joints, however, became uncomfortable, and she questioned if the sprays we put on apples were to blame. Eventually, we replaced most trees with sheep. Dad taught me how to care for newborn lambs, drive a tractor, and plant crops. He also showed me how to trap possums, an invasive pest that, while popular in Australia, poses a threat to native New Zealand animals and regularly eats our fruit. When we had a particularly terrible run of possums, Dad grabbed his single-shot .22 rifle.

I sat awake, watching Dad walk out into the darkness. "Can I come with you?" I offered. Possums startled me; they would occasionally appear outside my bedroom window, their huge eyes flashing in the darkness. Their raspy rasp sounded like a heavy smoker. But I was willing to put all that aside if it meant being helpful.

"Not until you learn how to use a gun carefully and properly," Dad replied as he walked out into the night. Soon after, dad taught me how to use the rifle. He set up a target and demonstrated how to hold the gun against my shoulder and maintain balance when it threw me back. It didn't matter how many times I fired; each one scared me. But I stuck with it, determined to learn.

I performed a number of things in those days that would have classified me as a "tomboy." I whizzed around the orchard on Dad's old Honda motorcycle, my mother shaking her head at my speed and warning my dad, "She's not taking that out on the road, Ross." One afternoon, I watched Dad inspect the undercarriage of our enormous, secondhand riding lawn mower, which had broken down for the third time that year. I stood on the loose gravel at the edge of the large corrugated iron structure, certain that Dad could fix it. He lay on the hot concrete floor of the shed, squirming uneasily, a confused expression on his face. Dad stretched one arm and requested me to pass him the wrench. I dashed over to the rusted toolbox, as if I were on a deadline.

"Thanks," he replied. He kept his gaze fixed on the bottom of the mower as he said, "You're the closest thing I have to a son."

Dad was already wrestling with a bolt by the time his remarks were finished. It's the closest thing dad has to a son. Dad has never admitted that he felt a void where a son should be. But I had always imagined that every parent desired a son. Didn't they? However, it appears that I do not need to worry. Whatever hole may have been, I was filling it. His daughter. Before long, I was beaming as I stood just beyond the shed's shade, my face turned toward the sun. I was useful. And that made me very proud.

Around that time, I had a fever and began throwing up. After a few days, I was so unwell that my parents made me sleep on the foldout couch on the mezzanine level so they could keep an eye on me, which they had never done before.

As I went in and out of sleep, the scenes around me changed. When I opened my eyes, the light ached so badly that Mum hurriedly closed the blinds. In the reduced light, I'd fall asleep again, only to wake up with my father by my side, his palm on my forehead. The next time I opened my eyes, Mum was lifting my head to assist me drink.

Dots erupted all over my skin. After three nights of fever and vomiting, my father grabbed me off the couch and brought me downstairs to the car. My mother placed her beloved just-in-case empty ice cream tub in my hands, and my parents drove me to the doctor for the second time, where I remained holding the tub during the exam.

I was too unwell to pay attention to what the doctor was saying, but I did interrupt him by vomiting into the container. My father returned me to the car, while my mother waited long enough for the doctor to advise her to drive me home and that I would be fine.

But I was not. Days have gone. At night, I slept close to Mum and Dad. During the day, they'd place me on the downstairs couch to keep an eye on me. I was lying there, half a stone lighter and thirsty after vomiting, when I heard a harsh, resolute voice. "Where is she then?"

My grandmother stood in the doorway, her tight gray locks and a cardigan draped over a blouse. Her huge glasses sat on the edge of her nose. "There you are," she said, her voice sharp. Even with my eyes half closed, I noticed something in her hand. "Your mother says you haven't been drinking enough." An untouched mug of grape juice and a spoon sat next to the couch. Nana laid the case down, perched on the side of the couch, and lifted the mug. My grandmother was not the type of woman to disobey.

I gently lifted my head, allowing her to spoon purple liquid into my mouth. She informed me about the necessity of staying hydrated, and in her voice, I could sense concern mixed with annoyance: either I shouldn't be sick, or I shouldn't be this sick. "There you go then, dear." When I finished, she nodded, pleased. "I have something here for you," she said. She picked up the black case. It was a hard shell, covered with aged leather, with two rusted locks and a tattered handle. She flicked the latches to open the case. I attempted to sit up, but all I could see inside was a dark brown violin.

"This was my mother's," she explained, carefully pulling it out and holding it up for me to see better. Two of the cords remained attached; the rest were broken and dangling. The inside of the case was lined with yellow spotted paper, and I noticed a name inscribed: McRae. This was my great grandmother's maiden name. The woman who arrived from Scotland with just her son, a pistol, and a violin.

The violin.

"I want you to look after this," Nana said. I'd been learning the violin for quite some time at this point. Not that I was really skilled. I had never learned to read music. I played by ear and learned the pieces by heart.

I couldn't understand why Nana was giving me one of her prized items at that moment. Perhaps she sensed I was sicker than the doctors thought. If so, she was correct: I would soon be hospitalized and diagnosed with Kawasaki disease, a rare pediatric ailment that causes inflammation of the blood vessels. I'd spend a week in that hospital bed, then another few weeks regaining my strength.

All I knew was that the violin was the most beautiful and unique gift I had ever received. I wanted Nana to understand how grateful I was and how important she had made me feel. But my eyes were really heavy. I closed them, and when I opened them again, Nana was gone.

CHAPTER 4

Morrinsville College, the lone high school in town, was only a few streets from my intermediate school, but with approximately 600 students scattered across five classes, it felt like a completely different planet. Louise had been there two years. At fifteen, she had long brown hair, long legs that made her a graceful jazz ballet dancer, and intelligence that propelled her to the top of most of her classes. I believed she had a slight rebellious streak. She rolled up her uniform skirt for starts. All of this made Louise the ideal person to bombard with questions as we approached my first day: where do third-graders sit? Can I say hi if I see you? What about Mum? Can I go to the canteen whenever I want? Mum had spent the last few years managing the school canteen, a tiny room buried beneath the school hall stocked with muesli bars, potato chips, meat pies, and sausage rolls.

Each morning, as Mum arrived to find pallets of meat pies ready, I made my way to the area outside the science building. I'd find my friends hanging around, waiting for the bell to sound. In the warmer months, we'd sit on the benches that ran beside the classrooms and sip on Juicies, which were frozen plastic tubes of tropical fruit juice. By the time the June cold hit, we were shivering, pulling up our long white slouch socks to keep our legs warm against the moist air.

Theo, I thought. Theo, Fiona's brother, is intelligent, beautiful, and extremely humorous. Who is quiet like my sister, has model airplanes on his shelves and band stickers on his dresser, eats Nutella right out of the jar, and occasionally wears a cheeky smirk. Theo. The faintest fog hung over the fields in the distance, moist and silent. Theo, Fiona's brother, murdered himself.

I took a deep breath and knocked on the door as I entered. The upstairs living area was crowded with adults. More adults gathered around the black lacquered dining table, and even more were in the kitchen. Their voices were murmurs, and their features were blurred. Stephen's face emerged from the blur. He motioned to the back of the home. "The girls are in their room," he replied simply.

As I passed Theo's room, everything looked the same as it always did: the gridline wallpaper, the green desk chair, and the stickers, some of which were partly scraped off, as if Theo had changed his mind about having them there in the first place. Vicky must have chosen the cheerful flowered drapes for him. School books were strewn on the shelf.

Theo's room, with his belongings.

I could hear the television in the girls' room playing a daytime show. I pushed open the door and placed my bag in the opening. Fiona and Penelope turned around. Fiona's hair lay damp against her cheeks, and her eyes were red and puffy. I opened my mouth but found myself speechless. Until now, everything about our friendship had been basic and straightforward. We had spent time together playing, hiking, dancing, and watching movies. We had sang silly songs, read Cleo magazine, talked Jim Morrison, listened to the Smashing Pumpkins, and pretended to be adults. Despite this, we were only children.

Fiona asked to spend the night at my house. Her home was overcrowded, overwhelming, and unhappy. Fiona asked about my religion for the first time as we were lying quietly in the darkness of my bedroom. Where I believed individuals went after they died. I told her what I believed to be true: that there was a God and an afterlife. A place where we can see our relatives again. I told her this because I believed it and it seemed like the appropriate thing to say. I wondered how anyone could get through anything like this.

But a few days later, I was at Fiona's house, right before Theo's burial, when a visitor mentioned God over lunch. Vicky was in the process of bringing soup and bread, and while I can't remember what the guest said, I remembered them attempting to console Fiona in the same manner that I had.

Vicky laid her ladle down on the table as soon as God was mentioned. "God?" she inquired. Her voice was sharp and forceful, but it quivered as she spoke. "If there is a God, how could He take my son? "How can he...?"

Instead of finishing, Vicky slammed her fist down on the black lacquered table, causing the forks and knives to jump as she choked back a shriek. Nobody looked at one other during the tense stillness that followed. My thoughts began to race, searching for an answer to her query. How could God exist?

I had always been a faithful member of my church. I'd never doubted God's existence or the veracity of the faith that had been a part of my family since Nana first spoke with Mormon missionaries years before I was born. The only thing I had ever questioned was the strength of my faith.

I was always taught that everything that happened was part of God's plan. If you couldn't answer a question within your beliefs, you simply weren't intended to grasp it. That modest viewpoint had sufficed. Until now.

I recall thinking, "I still believe in you, God." But I don't get this. I'll never comprehend this.

CHAPTER 5

I remember hearing a joke at school when I was about ten. Across the throng of students overflowing into the hallway after class, a girl my age cried "Hey!" to no one and everyone at the same time. She waited until she was sure at least a few kids were listening before beginning her impromptu comedy routine. "What's the difference between a Mormon and a Lada?"

To grasp the setup and punchline of this joke, you must first know something that few ten-year-olds knew: Lada was a brand of inexpensive, state-manufactured Russian cars with a reputation for erratic functionality. I was not aware of this. I'm not sure if any of the youngsters surrounding me knew. But, of course, whatever a Lada is wasn't the purpose. This was a Mormon joke, and I am Mormon.

The girl waited a beat before declaring triumphantly, "You can shut the door on a Mormon!".

I doubt she knew what she was saying. She was a kind youngster who let me play her Guns N' Roses tapes and was probably certainly repeating something she had heard. However, the joke's premise—that Mormons go door-to-door to promote their religion—was correct. While the joke did not make anyone laugh, it did have an impact in one way: it instilled in me a phobia of door knocking.

However, by the time I was about thirteen years old, it was my turn to knock on doors on God's behalf. I have conflicting views about this. On the one hand, I've always felt that religion was personal and individual. The closest I recall addressing it with anyone outside of my family was that night at my house with Fiona. However, there were other valid reasons to knock on the door.

As the missionaries approached each door, I stood back, watching and listening. Often no one responded. If someone did respond, the elders usually began with the same greeting: Hello, sir/ma'am. We represent the Church of Jesus Christ of Latter-day Saints. Often, that's when the conversation quickly ends. You can close the door on a Mormon.

When the door didn't close immediately, I'd move a little closer. I'd listen and see if I had anything to say. But no matter how difficult it seemed, I persisted, ignoring my strong desire to skip residences, even though every door felt like Lincoln Street with a rottweiler behind the fence.

A doorstep provides a glimpse into the outskirts of someone else's life. Scattered tennis shoes and upside-down gumboots by the back door reveal who lives inside, while toys and schoolbags at the entrance indicate how the day has gone.

While I struggled to initiate talks about God and, on occasion, politics, I discovered that if I was present to question someone about their life and what would make a difference in their lives, I could do so. That is what I wanted to do. I could speak with the mother whose home was so badly ventilated that condensation streaked down the inside of her windows and her children were ill. I could sit down with the man who had just moved off the streets and into his first home and talk about how the joy of shelter was balanced by the pain of loneliness. In fact, I could do these things without hesitation. On those future doorsteps, I would not only ask, but also share ideas that had been translated into legislation, policies that could potentially solve a problem. And once I accomplished that, there was no need to hold back.

Learning to door knock as a teenager provided additional rewards. It made all other cold-calling feel less intimidating—like the afternoon before my fourteenth birthday, when my mother drove me downtown to look for work.

That day, I went home from school to find Mum waiting for me, still dressed in her canteen uniform of an apricot smock and a cream cardigan. She said, "Darling, it's time you got a job—a real one." Louise and I were no longer carrying flyers—the sheer amount had finally overwhelmed even my parents—so it was time to try something fresh. Louise worked at a produce business called the Vege Bin, and as my birthday approached, Mum decided I was also "old enough."

In my room, I took out an old blue folder with plastic pockets and began filling it with anything I could find: academic achievements, a pie contest trophy from a school fair, and an award for my lamb at Calf Club Day. Everything was utterly unimportant, but it ended up in the folder.

The Morrinsville commercial district is less than a kilometre. There are no malls or restaurant chains. Kids my age had few employment options: a Chinese takeaway, a fish-and-chip business, a burger bar, a stationery store, an appliance store, or a gift shop.

It was Friday afternoon. Shops were closed for the day. Meanwhile, takeaway shops were preparing for their busiest shifts of the week. As I walked across the street with my blue folder tucked under my arm, my stomach dropped. Was I seriously going to stroll into a shop and beg for a job? That seemed nearly as terrifying as knocking on doors with the missionaries.

Mum and I made our first visit at the Golden Kiwi, a Morrinsville landmark and family-run fish and chip business. Throughout those years, its decor had stayed nearly unchanged: fresh fish in the window, wood-paneled walls, red marbled Formica counters, and enormous wall menus. In the back of the establishment, a pair of swinging wooden saloon doors separated the kitchen from the sit-down restaurant, which had painted cinderblock walls, vinyl chairs, and red-checkered tablecloths. At the Golden Kiwi, $5 gets you an entire meal, including fish, chips, and a salad. If you were feeling fancy, you might opt for the fresh snapper. Regardless of what you ordered, you'd always come across a member of the Covich family, who had operated the restaurant for nearly 30 years.

My relief at gaining a job was quickly replaced by a new concern: what if I messed up? The Golden Kiwi may get very busy, particularly on Fridays. I imagined Grant working his way through a lengthy line of dockets, the phone ringing, and all those restless diners in the dining room. What if I lose my first shift job?

Mum had worked in a similar shop as a teenager, and she knew the fundamentals of what I would need to learn. When we arrived home, she disappeared into the kitchen, returning with a newspaper and half a cabbage. "Here." She opened a newspaper in the center and dropped the cabbage in front of me. "Practice wrapping this," she urged.

When I gazed at Mum blankly, she sat down on the floor, placed the cabbage in the center of the newspaper, and wrapped it with the precision of a gift—but without the ribbon or tape. The operation necessitated not only strong folding but also a precise high-speed flip to keep the cabbage from slipping out.

"There," Mum exclaimed with satisfaction. She sat back and admired her work. "Of course, with chips, you'll have to hold them carefully as you flip, or they'll pour out the front. Now you try."

I unwrapped the package and rearranged the cabbage in the center—a lousy alternative for chips, I thought. Even yet, it proved to be more difficult than expected. I didn't fold the paper securely enough, so when I went to flip it, the cabbage tumbled out the side and across the floor.

Mum offered me a reassuring grin. "Give it another try."

Wrap, unwrap, and repeat. Wrap, unwrap, and repeat. I rehearsed the maneuver thousands of times that night, occasionally pausing just long enough to consider how ludicrous the scene was. It was the night before my fourteenth birthday, and I was sitting on the floor of our lounge, continuously wrapping half a cabbage in newspaper. But even the ridiculousness of the circumstance did not deter me.

This, too—imagining every worst-case scenario and then feverishly attempting to prevent each one in turn—would be practice for a whole other kind of employment. I was already beginning to prepare for a role I could never have imagined, such as knocking on doors and presenting a folder to an almost stranger and asking them to place their trust in me.

Mr. Fountain was just in his twenties, yet he'd already lost almost all of his hair. He wore little round glasses and marched into class each day with the vigour of someone who has consumed one more cup of coffee than they should. For him, each session represented an opportunity to apply a new lesson. For example, he once reconfigured the classroom to resemble Parliament's floor. Or the day he taught us about Indian history by printing off two diametrically opposed pieces on Gandhi—one disparaging of the leader and the other celebrating his accomplishments—and urging us to "find out who he was." Find out for yourself. He wanted us to learn to make our own decisions. Perhaps he wanted us to understand something else. Both people and history are difficult.

In 1995, when I was fifteen, the government apologized to Waikato Māori for violations of the Treaty of Waitangi and the ensuing Tainui Settlement, including cash reparations for land seizure. The first settlement between Māori and the government sparked significant controversy in the news. Reporters pressed microphones on people's faces in the street, asking if they felt settlements were a good idea. Many people might say, "Isn't that all in the past?" or We simply need to move on. There was a weird anxiety in these responses, as if acknowledging a wrong somehow made everyone complicit. Or perhaps they are less patriotic about their home. However, learning about New Zealand's history did not improve my feelings toward my home nation. In fact, it was in Mr. Fountain's class, lesson by lesson, that I discovered that appreciating where you were from entailed identifying all the flaws that needed to be corrected and all the ways that it could be improved.

While I enjoyed history, Louise excelled at chemistry, biology, arithmetic, and physics, all of which I struggled with. She has her creative outlet: photography. She purchased a 35mm camera and brought it everywhere. At family gatherings, Mom compelled us to pose, fiddling with the camera long after everyone had lost patience with her timer not working. There was an unused kitchen in the orchard cool-store shed, which my dad painted black and outfitted with $600 in old darkroom equipment they purchased during garage sales.

I adored assisting Louise in the darkroom. We'd stand together with the red light on, mixing chemicals and seeing images emerge, removing them from their chemical trays and hanging them around the room. The darkroom occasionally felt like our own world, much as a three-acre area of forest once did. Louise's photos also allowed me to delve deeper into our family history. After Nana died, we discovered some old negatives in her possessions, which Louise and I turned into prints.

During the 1990s, either the politics of the moment escalated, or I simply became more politically conscious. As I continued to observe, I began to offer my thoughts. And the more I did, the more conflicts I ended up having—including at my own dining table.

Fortunately, my strong opinions quickly found a more practical outlet. I realized I wasn't horrible at public speaking and won the school speech competition several years in a row. Eventually, at my mother's prodding, I entered further competitions. Although I enjoyed standing in front of people to share a story or an idea, the nerves associated with public speaking were almost crippling. From the time a competition was announced, I couldn't stop thinking about it. I slept poorly the night before each event, waking up every few moments to consider if I had adequately memorized my speech and what I would do if I lost my spot. By morning, my stomach was in such dreadful knots that I couldn't eat.

My solutions differed. I tried powerful mints before going on stage. I tried lemon water. I tried saying "lemon, lemon, lemon." My mother even went to the pharmacy and returned with a set of pastilles designed for chemotherapy patients whose salivary glands were injured. Nothing worked. If anything, my fixation made everything worse.

Surprisingly, I never wondered why I was so nervous. By all standards, I was a good speaker. I took the time to carefully prepare my arguments. I knew every speech so well that I rarely had to refer to the index card notes I took. I had won several school and regional accolades. But the reality was, I couldn't shake the feeling that something would go horribly wrong. And that if it did, it would be proof that I wasn't qualified to be there in the first place.

Mr. Fountain came closest to clarifying what was happening. He had participated in speech competitions in high school and had won the national UN competition in 1989. When I told him how nervous I was, he nodded thoughtfully. "You know, Jacinda," he said, "some days I stand up at the front of this classroom, convinced that someone is going to jump out from behind those desks and tell the whole room that I don't actually know what I'm doing." It took me a while to understand what he was saying. Mr. Fountain was the best teacher I have ever had. Nonetheless, what he was describing felt quite familiar. That's when Mr. Fountain said something I'll never forget.

He continued: "That feeling is called impostor syndrome."

I took it in. "Impostor syndrome." Two words that felt like puzzle parts clicking together. I immediately wondered why Mr. Fountain would ever have a problem like this, but I wasn't willing to give myself the same kindness. His worry was unreasonable, I reasoned, whereas mine was not. Still, the event offered great comfort. If Mr. Fountain felt the same way I did, and there were two of us, other individuals most likely did as well. Probably many individuals did; after all, the phenomena was named. None of this helped my rumbling stomach or dry mouth, but it did help me keep going. That's how I got the debate team's attention.

I was fifteen years old, in my third year of high school, when the debate team's "first speaker" was unable to attend a tournament, and the team requested me to step in for her. I'd seen the team several times and considered it far more fascinating than the monologues in speech competitions. The debate featured heated exchanges between speakers, quick-witted rebuttals, and even sanctioned interjections in which team members jumped to their feet and exclaimed, "Point of information!" Sitting in the crowd, I frequently found myself constructing arguments in my brain, as if I were already on stage.

That first event was regional, so we'd be playing against teams from schools all throughout the Waikato. My teammates, Anthea and Matthew, were two years my senior. Matthew rarely needed to rehearse his remarks, which he delivered with a somewhat plummy accent that belied his father's profession as a trucker. Anthea was careful and meticulous, able to dissect an argument piece by piece until nothing remained. My task was to set the team up. Lay out our main point, then return at the conclusion to make a closing statement in what was dubbed the "leader's reply."

I felt confident in my ability to debate from the beginning. I knew how to form and present an argument since I had gone back and forth with my parents, and the parents of my friends, on many matters. Because of my inclination to over-prepare and envisage every worst-case scenario, I was able to envision any possible argument that the opposite side would present to me. Until now, my near-constant anxiety had been crippling. It suddenly seemed like a superpower.

Debate would lead me to places I never anticipated. It would be my second plane ride. It would allow me to see both the South Island and the capital city. Through argument, I visited the New Zealand Parliament and attended formal functions and meals including "pepper-encrusted Brie"—whatever that is.

Did my mouth still dry up to the point that I couldn't say vowels? It did. Was I usually nervous? Always. Did my stomach suffer so terribly before each event that I couldn't eat breakfast? Yes. But it was also the first time I'd discovered something that had transformed what felt like crippling shortcomings into strengths. And it would not be the last.

CHAPTER 6

My Friday night shifts at the Golden Kiwi followed a consistent pattern. I arrived at 5:00 p.m. in my pale blue uniform, which hung just over my knees and featured a zipper running from the modest V-neck to just above the hem. Although it was once a nurse's outfit, I guessed it was worn in a nursing home cafeteria around 1980.

One Friday night during my junior year of high school, I had no intention of returning home as usual. Instead, I was going to a gathering called the "head boy and girl party." The head boy and girl were two of the most significant students at the school, elected by their peers and approved by teachers and administrators. Though the head boy and girl held official positions, such as class co-presidents, tonight's celebration was entirely unofficial—a tradition that included music, friends, and alcohol.

Hot Guy examined the menu. I studied him. He had a restless energy and shifted his weight from one foot to another. His eyes flickered frantically as he placed his order. I did my best to walk back to the kitchen with a fake disinterest. As I hung the docket above the vat, I heard Carol in the storeroom sorting boxes. And suddenly, behind me, I heard the ping of the till.

Wait. There is no one else there. As I returned to the doors, I noticed Hot Guy leaning over the counter and withdrawing cash with both hands. "He's robbing the till!" I yelled. Carol was at least a foot shorter and almost thirty years older than me, but she moved like lightning. She sped by me and was immediately on his track as he ripped open the front door and sprinted out.

"Give me back my money!" Carol ran after him. I also followed. Outside, he got into an ancient brown Triumph that was idling on the opposite side of the road. And then he was gone, around the corner too quickly for us to capture his license plate, leaving me and Carol in the center of the empty street, staring at the spot where the automobile had vanished.

It was late when police arrived and left. I drove home, changed out of my uniform, sprayed myself with Impulse body spray to mask the odor of fried food, and headed to the party with far less zest than before the heist.

The party was held at a student's house on the outskirts of town. Old automobiles parked on the grassy edge, while Metallica played from a set of speakers. It was busy behind the home, with kids in loose trousers and printed T-shirts drinking, sitting in plastic chairs, and leaning on hay bales. I spotted my friend Ginny across the yard. "You won't believe what happened tonight," I said.

Ginny and I had gotten friends years before while working on a research project that tested whether the sun faded denim faster than washing it. Ginny fit in better with the popular circle than I did. She was educated and studious, with strawberry-blond hair and athletic abilities. We sat down together, and I told her the story while we watched the kids move in groups through the darkness.

Hot Guy ended up going through the youth justice system. He repaid the money he took at a rate of $5 per week and apologized to Carol and Grant for it.

That was not the end of it for me, however. I thought about that night for months afterward. It wasn't the crime of the century, but did he seriously consider it before it happened? Why did he do this? Why would anyone? These were questions I had seen my father face. They are now also nagging me.

Mum had now moved closer to Dad. They exchanged deep stares, the kind couples have when a secret is unexpectedly revealed.

It took me a few moments to understand what that look meant. Just long enough for divergent memories of the past to click into place. Discomfort at my Nana's funeral. Following that, the family met. The unspoken gap among the family. And then there came the photograph of Grandfather Harry and the man carrying the swan. The man who looked just like my father—so much so that we were sure it was him. But it wasn't. It was Jim. The one who worked beside my grandfather. It was Jim.

Everything immediately made clear. My father's biological father was Jim.

I don't recall much of the chat after that. But in the years since, Dad would confirm that it was correct. No, he did not know the entire story. And when I asked him if this fact affected his feelings for his mother, he said no. It had not. However, it altered his feelings for Granddad Harry. "He must have known," my father stated. "But he didn't love me any less.... I loved and admired him even more for that." As he spoke, my grandfather—who had before appeared to be in the shadows—came into clear view. He was no longer simply sitting near the coal range; he was the reason it was running. The Christmas supper that materialized despite Nana's illness was not an indication of her miraculous recovery; rather, it was Harry.

After learning about Nana and Jim, I was upset—angry even—on behalf of everyone I felt had been harmed. My father, my aunts, uncles, and grandfather. And that was before I considered what the church may say about it. But now I realized that I wasn't just upset for other people. I was distressed about what it meant for me and my memories.

I wanted Nana to be the person I assumed I knew—and only that person. But until I learnt about Jim, it was as if my memory of her was fragmented. I hoped I could talk to Nana and ask her why, what had occurred, so that I could start putting those parts back where they should be.

But suddenly my strong questions were softening. Many items that had previously been black and white were blurring into gray. People were complicated. Lives were difficult. Why wouldn't that apply to my family too?

I sat on the floor, violin case in front of me. Opening it was like entering a time machine. There was the yellow lining with silver flecks, and the instrument's bent wood. Nana informed me that a student of Stradivari, the finest violin maker of all time, crafted the violin. It had journeyed by sea over twelve thousand miles from Scotland to New Zealand, passing down from my great-grandmother to Nana to me. I was now its caretaker, and it was time to have the violin fixed.

I felt very sorry. I documented the entire awful scenario in my diary, torn between whether or not to proceed with the violin repair and being devastated by the loss. Beyond that, there was a deeper question: Did this new understanding alter my feelings for the violin? Sure, others could value it less, but did I?

And what about Nana? Were my childhood recollections of her any less real because her narrative seemed more convoluted to me now? Was it the fresh things I'd learnt that characterized her? Or could I simply cling on to the person I'd known for as long as I had?

A few days later, I contacted the repair shop. "Go ahead and repair the violin, please," I told you. Yes, the violin was not an antique. But it remained a family treasure.

CHAPTER 7

As I approached high school graduation, I had a decision to make. What would I do with my life? I agonized over this question. I was confident that whichever step I made next would permanently establish me on my current course.

Over the years, I examined several vocations, including attorney, juvenile aid officer in the police force, and counselor. These were useful jobs. They aided others and, maybe more importantly, made them feel accessible. However, I was still unsure. So, before deciding on a career, I contemplated pursuing a bachelor of arts degree, which would allow me to study subjects I enjoyed, such as history and politics. But when I told my parents about this plan, Dad said, "Well, you better learn to ask, 'Do you want fries with that?' because that's the only job you'll get with an arts degree."

Dad was not being nasty. I understood it even if I rolled my eyes at him. He only wanted me to have job security, like he had throughout his decades-long career. My sister and I would be the first in our family to go to university. Higher education seemed to have become a costly privilege. If I took out a loan for tuition or living expenses, the interest would start accruing immediately—before I even graduated—at a rate of roughly 7%. I wasn't sure I'd ever make enough money to pay off the loans. I wanted a decent job, a consistent job, but there was a significant chance I wouldn't stay there long enough to be well compensated. After all, I'd ultimately marry and have children, and who knows what would become of my work after that.

My sister was already engaged to her boyfriend, Warren, whom she met at church. I liked Warren. He was shy, quiet, and quite kind to Louise. I was happy for her, even though I was secretly sad that my near-constant companion and closest confidante was leaving. But her participation confirmed what I had long believed: that success required having a family. The only thing I was certain of about myself was that I enjoyed politics. By now, I'd seen two elections and knew I was firmly on the side of the Labour Party, which my grandmother had always backed.

Even as I stated this, I still didn't know what I wanted to do. I assumed my most likely career path would be management communications, working for an in-house communications team in a private sector organization. Was I excited by this? Not really. But I'd heard there were jobs in the neighborhood; wasn't that sufficient? It was far more opportunity than my mother had ever had.

My whole life, I'd seen Mum prioritize everyone else's needs before her own. She has worked at the canteen for over seven years. And even after all these years, she made less per hour than I did as a cashier at Countdown. But only once do I recall her indicating that she might have desired anything else. We'd been talking about her long-held dream of becoming an accountant. It would have been so rewarding, she remarked, to show me I could.

Harry Duynhoven was a member of Parliament, representing New Plymouth, which is where my aunty Marie lived. She'd volunteered for his campaigns and was always proud of his large majority, especially in a district where Labour had won only five of the previous twenty elections. Harry had gained the district's trust by campaigning against issues that irritated him, such as used-car dealers who were reselling imported vehicles.

Jenny Shipley, the National Party's leader and New Zealand's first female prime minister, led the government at the time. In New Zealand, there is only one lawmaking body, Parliament, and forming a government requires at least half of the seats. The leader of the largest party becomes Prime Minister. For nearly a decade, the conservative National Party has led the government. However, after the 1996 election, they needed the cooperation of New Zealand First, a populist party led by Winston Peters, to create a majority. That partnership had just disintegrated, and people appeared to be tired of the cuts imposed to public services.

In 1999, it appeared that Labour would finally have a chance to win. If they did, Helen Clark, the Labour leader with decades of experience and a sharp mind, would become the new prime minister.

"I'm wondering if you'd like to come down to New Plymouth for a bit," Harry went on: "to help with the campaign."

I sat bolt upright on the staircase. Just five minutes ago, I was urgently attempting to focus on linguistics while wondering if it was too early to go to bed. Now I was speaking with an MP, who, strangely, appeared to believe I could be beneficial.

Harry started detailing some of the chores he needed help with. Recruit volunteers through phone calls and door-to-door outreach as the campaign grows. "And of course on Election Day we need help with getting out the vote, driving people to the polls, scrutineering," the politician went on.

My thoughts raced. In my eighteen years, I'd mastered a variety of skills, including how to prune trees, wrap fish and chips, and ring up groceries, none of which would likely come in handy during a campaign. Also, I was not from New Plymouth. Mine was a dairy town. New Plymouth was primarily an energy hub, with thousands of people working directly and indirectly in the oil and gas business. I know nothing about those difficulties.

Then then, I understood how to knock on people' doors and begin talking to them. I know how to work hard without stopping. And if I could help Harry, it meant I could also help Helen Clark, the Labour Party's leader, win the election. It meant giving Labour the opportunity to change all of the things I had noticed that didn't feel right. That means raising the minimum wage, increasing workers' rights, and preventing students from accruing additional school debt. It meant doing something.

In the end, I raised the only criticism I could completely describe. "My aunty is away," I explained. Marie had accepted a position as a casino waitress in Australia. It paid well, even if it was beginning to take its toll on her petite frame. The large platters she lifted high over her head or balanced across her forearms were causing damage to her shoulder cartilage. It seemed inevitable that she would return home; I just didn't know when. In the meantime, I didn't know anyone in New Plymouth, a three-hour trip away, and I didn't have enough money to pay for lodging.

In New Zealand, the campaign to elect a government and prime minister is short but intense. Each election must be held within three years of the previous one, but the election date is otherwise determined by the prime minister, who carefully chooses a Saturday depending on factors such as school holidays and rugby games. Parliament adjourns four to seven weeks before Election Day, and MPs begin their campaigning.

When Harry's campaign manager called me a few days later, he requested that I arrive as soon as possible—well before the campaign began. They needed someone to recruit volunteers so they could start right away when the campaign began. He advised that this volunteer recruitment take place over my university break. So I swapped shifts at the store, loaded my mother's Toyota Corona, and headed the road. The route to New Plymouth consists of long lengths of tiny winding roads punctuated by the occasional one-way bridge and steep valley. Mum's Corona had only four speeds, and it grumbled every time it passed 90 km/h, as if it wished for a fifth gear. The old tape player had a long black line dangling from it to which I hooked my Discman. During the three-hour journey, I sung along to The Smashing Pumpkins, Tripping Daisy, and Portishead, and when the Discman died, I switched to a strange a cappella version of "Bohemian Rhapsody." I had a large map in the passenger seat, but I knew where the major turnoffs were. Past the tourist draw that is the glowworm caverns, via little rural communities, till I reach the west coast, with its craggy shorelines and waves breaking along the road.

For the next three weeks, I worked at both Lorna's house and the Labour Party headquarters, a modest timber facility that resembled an old community hall. Phoebe, Harry's electorate agent, sat to the right as you entered, assisting with casework. If a person had a problem, such as receiving unemployment benefits or dealing with immigration issues, they might seek assistance from their local MP. Phoebe was available to assist Harry in his workplace.

Campaigns require volunteers. A lot of people volunteered. They're needed for leaflet distribution, door knocking, phone canvassing, and voter turnout on Election Day. Without volunteers, campaigns fail or never take off. The Labour Party has thousands of members; the difficulty is to turn them into volunteers at election time. And it was my responsibility to encourage supporters to devote their time and energy to getting Harry elected. My instruments were a large white portable landline phone, dozens of pages of an Excel spreadsheet containing hundreds of names and phone numbers, and Lorna's constant encouragement.

On the first day, I sat at Lorna's dining room table, complete with a white crocheted tablecloth, while she wandered around the small kitchen nearby. I positioned a blank piece of paper at the bottom of the first row of the spreadsheet to align the name with the phone number, took a deep breath, and began dialing.

"Hi, my name is Jacinda Ardern, and I'm calling on behalf of Harry Duynhoven." By the end of day one, I had a script written. Not all calls were uncomplicated. The listings were three years old. Sometimes things changed dramatically, and I discovered I had an unusual ability to make those changes as awkward as possible. I asked someone if they could deliver pamphlets, only to discover that they could no longer walk. When someone told me they couldn't leave their house, I offered they join our phone bank, where "we'd provide the call sheets," unaware that they were also extremely visually challenged. Several times, I wanted to talk with someone who had died since the last election. I made careful notes, hoping that no future caller would make the same mistakes I did.

Sitting in that first meeting, discussing the plan for the following several months, I felt like I was part of a team—the important back end that enabled all of the large, public events to take place. This gave me all the motivation I needed to continue with the laborious task of making calls.

Near the conclusion of week one, I began to feel like an old hand. I dialed a number, like I had done hundreds of times before, and prepared to repeat the script I now knew by memory. As the phone rang, I double-checked the name on the spreadsheet in front of me.

A familiar monologue of doubt began playing in my mind, questioning whether I should be there, doing that job. Lorna stepped in, and my head was on the table. "You okay?" she inquired. I informed Lorna about the John Young phone call. To my amazement, she threw her head back and laughed—a full-body chuckle, like I'd expect from my irreverent aunty Marie.

I kept going through the bundles of paper, my fingers double-checking each name after the next. Peter…Graham…Susan. Election Day, phone canvassing, and leaflets. Disconnected number… I'm too unwell… DNC… The stack shrank, while the list of campaign volunteers became greater.

One day, at the end of my volunteer recruitment phase, I was entering names from recent phone calls into a spreadsheet at the Labour Party offices when I heard the door open. I glanced out from behind the doorframe to see if anyone was there when I heard Phoebe's calm voice. "Hello! "How can I help you?"

An old man stood in the doorway. He wore a faded parka over worn pants. His shoes appeared to be at least a decade old, and his face was covered with white stubble. He shuffled wearily into Phoebe's office, where I overheard him telling her his story. He was a granddad. His grandson resided with him. The boy attended school but had bad asthma. He wasn't well enough to work, and he was dealing with the costs of caring for a granddaughter, their home, and illness. He suspected that the house was making them both ill.

In other words, for all Phoebe's hard work and good intentions to truly improve this man's life, the system must change. That meant the government needed to reform.

That afternoon, after finishing my sheets for the day, I packed up and said goodbye to Phoebe. I had been at New Plymouth for over a fortnight. But seeing this man and hearing his story brought home the importance of this election, or any election. An election was more than just a televised contest. It wasn't just phone calls or pages from an Excel spreadsheet. It was about actual events that happened to real individuals. If Harry won—if Labour won—real people's lives might improve.

I got into the car and tossed my papers on the passenger side. As I turned on the Corona, I had another thought. What may it be like? To not just aid people one-on-one—as a good community member and volunteer, as my mother had done her entire life—but also to have a vote and a voice in the place that made and modified the laws.

Marie arrived in New Plymouth over twenty years ago as a newly divorced single mother with two children. There was a housing crisis at the time, so she and her children spent three months living in a camper van while she looked for a place to reside. Every day, she'd leave the kids off at school and go to the housing corporation office, hoping that they could help. They eventually moved her to public housing in Marfell, one of New Plymouth's worst neighbourhoods.

Every district has areas that appear to be easier to campaign in. Flat suburban streets with practically everyone already enrolled and planning to vote. But those were the places my aunty Marie placed at the bottom of her list.

Marie has been working on Labour initiatives for several years. Her first campaign was with my grandmother in the 1970s, when Helen Clark ran for the Piako seat. Marie had amazing stories from years of door-to-door campaigning. Like the time she assumed she was surrounded by Labour fans because "everyone wore red" until she realized it was the color of the local gang. But Marie wasn't one to put a story aside. If she noticed someone in need, she would act immediately.

Years ago, when door-knocking in Marfell, she came across a woman whose home had a hole in virtually every wall, no heat, a damaged toilet, a broken shower, and a stove that she described as "buggered." Marie returned; she continued to visit, developing a relationship with the woman. Marie eventually assisted the woman in obtaining assistance and repairing her home, which included patching holes, repairing the shower and toilet, redoing the kitchen, pulling up carpets, and varnishing the flooring. New curtains and drapes. Painted both inside and out.

Aunty Marie taught me how to shake gates when I arrived at a new residence. Just shake it, she explained on our first day. If there is a dog, it will come out, and you will know if it wants a bit of you. Most of the time, they are OK. In truth, you should be concerned about the minor issues. I've never been bitten. Go ahead, sweetheart. Give it a small shake. So I would shake boldly and purposefully, thinking that my rattling would protect me.

Meanwhile, everyone I'd been contacting to get involved was banding together and utilizing the structured campaign machinery: leaflet distribution, phone canvassing, and door knocking on weekdays and weekends.

It did not take long to have the advertisement up and running. I occasionally heard it while driving around town. Then, one afternoon, while I was driving back to Marie's, I heard not just the advertisement, but also the broadcasters discussing it. They were still talking about it when I returned to Marie's, so I got out of the car, walked across the street to the station, and approached the open window of the booth. I noticed two young males with headphones and microphones sitting in front of them. I stuck my head through the window. Only briefly second-guessing myself, I greeted them.

"Hi! "My name is Jacinda," I said. "I'm the one who voiced that ad." The announcers brought a microphone closer to me, and I found myself participating in a live radio conversation. I don't remember exactly what I said, but I do remember how much I enjoyed that moment: being able to communicate something so important to me and something I believe every young person should care deeply about, all while putting my head awkwardly through a window.

I paid close attention to every aspect of the campaign. I read publications and policy announcements, anticipating questions about issues when knocking on doors. I attended neighborhood meetings and was familiar with area unemployment and benefit statistics, average home costs, and the availability of state housing. I didn't want to be just a volunteer; I wanted to be a resource for any information an indecisive voter would require.

I also realized how much personal connection is to people. In New Plymouth, everyone knew Harry. When people realized I was there on Harry's behalf, they frequently had a tale to tell. Harry had visited their business or school. He had assisted them in moving into their new home. I once visited a house and discovered the owner kneeling in the front garden. after she realized why I was there, she jumped up from her weeding and approached me to tell me that after her husband died a few years ago, Harry gave her a card. She had it on her mantel for months. She wasn't sure how Harry knew about her loss, but it was important to her that he know.

As we walked from home to house, Marie and I, like other volunteers, kept thorough records of which people claimed they were likely to vote Labour in the booth. On Election Day, we knew we'd want to check in with these supporters to ensure they went to the polls. If they hadn't, we'd make every effort to get them there. In a small country like ours, seats can be won or lost with fewer than five votes—or even one.

By the last week of the campaign, I could feel my aunty getting tired. Right, darling, I'm starting the day with only a black coffee. But after lunch, we'll return here. I'm preparing you one of my large sandwiches. Sprouts, beetroot, all that delicious stuff. We need to maintain our strength up. She'd sit for a bit, an Arcoroc glass mug in hand, steam rising from her fresh instant coffee. A few minutes later, we'd be out the door.

On Election Day, Aunty Marie and I got up early. The nearest polling booth was just around the corner, but we chose to drive. Marie knew we had a busy day ahead of us, and that "we'll be buggered by the end of it all." We parked across the street from New Plymouth Boys High School, an airy, Edwardian-style edifice made of roughcast concrete. As we walked inside, the weather seemed turbulent and foreboding.

We entered a vast meeting hall. I collected my ballot from a trestle table, proceeded to the cardboard booth, grabbed my giant orange marker, and voted Labour.

Within hours, the news got better. Labor had defeated the National Party. That meant Helen Clark, Labour's leader, would succeed Jenny Shipley as prime minister.

I reflect on this now, and I realize how incredible it was that in my short life, I was able to witness not just one woman ascend to the highest office in the country, but two. Because of them, I never thought my gender would stop me from participating in politics. Or that it was impossible to be both a woman and a leader. But what personality did you need? That was a totally different tale. That was the end of my campaign and political involvement for the time being.

It was time to focus on my academics and seek a career.

CHAPTER 8

The rizona was hot, lovely, and pricey. I had saved enough money to survive there, but not enough to live independently. I lived in Mesa, about eight miles from college, with a freshly married Mormon friend named Alys, whom I had met through missionaries in New Zealand, her husband, Dale, and their hairless cat, which looked like something out of Dr. Evil's lair. Alys and Dale resided in a split-level house with an open floor layout on a large suburban street.

Everything was flat and low-rise, except for Camelback Mountain, which glowed red in the distance. The desert environment was very different from what I was used to. Most front yards were covered in stone and littered with succulents, including giant yucca spikes and cacti that stood taller than me. Towering gates encircled backyards, yet I couldn't envision kids playing outside. Not in that heat. In some places, there were no sidewalks, which made sense. Nobody here walked. Even when I tried, people honked at me, as if to tell me that this was a poor idea.

This loneliness went deeper than homesickness. It was about much more than the distance between Arizona and New Zealand, the change of scenery, or the fact that long-distance phone calls were too expensive for me to call Mum or Dad frequently. It was more fundamental. I'd come here hoping that Arizona would help me bridge the growing gap between my principles and my religion. But it hadn't; if anything, the disparity had become more prominent. And I still hadn't found anyone or anything that could help. Why was I there? I had no idea. I had always felt that every experience had a reason and purpose. But when I finished my sandwich and packed up in the scorching red sun to go to my next lesson, I couldn't figure out what the point of this one was.

A few weeks into the semester, I awoke to the news on my clock radio. Typically, the newscasters tried to ease us into the day by talking about sports and the weather. But today, they were discussing something different. In my half-sleep, I remembered the words "plane...tower...fire." I sat upright. Terrible situation in New York City. The World Trade Center. An accident, perhaps.

After a nearly empty bus trip, I arrived at university, astonished and silent. Nobody was on the street. The campus was almost vacant. Even the sky was calm. ASU is adjacent to Phoenix Sky Harbor Airport. I'd grown accustomed to commercial flights buzzing overhead that I stopped noticing them. Their unexpected departure, the stillness above, was unnerving.

On that particular day, nearly all classes were suspended. However, it is not all. My American foreign policy class would go ahead. I had shown up knowing that my professor expected us to. I sat in the front row and silently pulled out my books. My professor stepped into the classroom, saying he recognized that several students had questioned whether class should continue. However, the terrorists, he reminded us, intended us to modify our behavior in response to their actions. "Well, fuck them," he replied.

It was only hours after the attack, but my professor's pointed defiance would soon be everywhere, blending with a tremendous wall of patriotism unlike anything I had ever seen before. The patriotism I'd known back home came through in simple ways: we showed off our landscapes to overseas friends, beamed with joy at the sight of a Kiwi on the world stage, or welled up when we saw the haka—a traditional Māori call to arms that symbolized strength, unity, and mana (or pride). Flags were not common in New Zealand. We did not hold our hands to our chests during the national anthem. Our patriotism was different.

However, we hadn't only lost hundreds of individuals in one awful catastrophe.

In the weeks and months following September 11, I witnessed patriotism become a means of demonstrating that the American spirit had not been broken. Flags were no longer just flapping atop poles in public areas and yards; they were also hanging from windows, emblazoned on T-shirts, printed on paper, and affixed to bus windows and drugstore automated doors.

I walked the terrain, trying to make sense of everything. I was continually watching the news, hoping to gain a deeper understanding of what the world had just witnessed and what was happening in reaction. I watched American leaders on TV. I heard them claim that these acts of mass murder were intended to scare our country into disarray and retreat, and that America was targeted because it is the brightest symbol of freedom. However, these sentences did not address the question that was building in my mind—and that I imagined would be answered at some point by someone.

I was in communication class when I made the mistake of asking the question myself. Near the end of class, my professor urged students to reflect on their feelings. After a few minutes, an athletic male from the back of the class raised his hand. He said since the attack he has been unable to look at "an Arab person" without thinking if they are a terrorist. I had turned to listen to the student, but as soon as he said this, I whirled around to look at the professor, ready for him to reprimand him: You cannot criticize an entire community based on the conduct of a few. Or, you can criticize violent extremism without condemning an entire population. Instead, the professor was nodding along.

I did remain silent—in that class and for the remainder of the semester. I studied hard. I turned in my writings on time. I still felt lonely. I had yet to address the tension between my principles and my beliefs. But somewhere along the way, my sense of purposelessness faded. Perhaps I now had a cause to be there, under the burning heat. Maybe I was there to listen. To watch. Observe. I wasn't sure why. I would not know for long. I just had a feeling: the world had changed, and it was critical to pay attention.

CHAPTER 9

When you run for Parliament, you have a choice: stand out front, be the salesperson for great ideas. You'll put yourself up, beg for votes, and say, "This is why I should be your MP." You are decisive, confident, and eager to take the stage.

Perhaps for some people it is. However, it is possible that not everyone experiences this. Perhaps the decision occurs in such small increments that it never feels like a decision at all. Perhaps you will say no at first. Perhaps you said no more than once. You can say no as many times as you like. Sometimes it happens anyhow. At least that's how it went for me.

The first call arrived on a frigid day in late 2007, two years after I had left the Beehive. I was on an ice rail platform in South London, watching two Australians balance a BBQ grill on wheels. It'd been a year of transition. Just months ago, I'd seen Tony Blair's final speech to Parliament. In the United States, Barack Obama, a progressive senator from Illinois, announced his candidacy for president.

But on this particular day, my thoughts were more ordinary, such as whether the tube's District line, the green line, would be—unusually—on time. I felt a vibration in my coat pocket from my Nokia phone. I dug it out, my fingers burned from the cold, and discovered the caller's name: Phil Goff.

Huh. Phil never phoned me.

When I left New Zealand for New York City, I couch surfed with a buddy, volunteered at a home care workers' union and a soup kitchen, and depleted my finances far more quickly than I had anticipated. That's when I packed my belongings and traveled to London, where I was legally allowed to work.

I received a job as a policy adviser at the Cabinet Office's Better Regulation Executive, a title that would end most polite conversations. I'd even begun shortening what I told people I did. One day, I arrived home to my Fulham flat, which I shared with two other New Zealanders. Our upstairs neighbor was sitting on the front step, enjoying some rare British sunshine. We started conversing, and when he asked what we did for work, I told him I worked in the Cabinet Office. "Oh, right," he responded with a heavy Australian accent, nodding his head. There was a pause. "What type of cabinets do you make?" He was not being cheeky; his query was genuine.

"Dining and occasional," I answered. I smiled and let him sunbathe.

I traveled a lot, but not like most people do. I volunteered for the International Union of Socialist young, a century-old organization that represents the young sections of socialist parties worldwide. I would advance from vice president to president, becoming the first woman in my region to achieve this status.

I'd ignored New Zealand politics. Up till now.

I hadn't communicated with Phil in years. By this point, he was in the process of finalizing the world's first free trade agreement with China, which was not without controversy at home. I knew he was busy. So, why is he calling me now? And how late? It was after ten p.m. in Wellington.

Our conversation started with casual conversation. Yes, it was cold now. Yes, I still like living in London. My sister had a terrific job and now resided in London. She and Warren had split, but she was still happy and active. I'd made many friends here. I adored working as a civil worker. I was still traveling extensively with the International Union of Socialist Youth, much as Helen Clark had in the 1970s. In other words, all was well. How was it in Wellington?

Phil cut to the chase. "Look, we need some young candidates," he told me.

There it was, the identical suggestion I had heard back in Wellington. This time, however, it was more straightforward. Phil didn't recommend that I run eventually. He asked me to run in the 2008 election. Next year.

Labour had been suffering from the third-term blues, which appeared to affect every political party in New Zealand after eight years in office. Since the last election, the National Party has made substantial gains. Their new leader, John Key, was a professional investment banker who appeared reasonable and friendly. He had a lot of momentum, having surpassed Labour in the polls by more than 10 points a year before the election.

"We definitely need more young people, and we need more women," Phil said afterwards. "Would you consider coming home? "To run?"

The day was London drab, one of those mornings when I knew there would only be a few hours of acceptable daylight. But in my mind, I was back in the car with Phil in 2002, driving through verdant suburban streets on our way to the airport following a challenging public meeting. He informed me that day that if they ever asked me to flee, I should not do it.

Now I was watching my train draw in. The doors slid open. I stood motionless as one of the Australians stepped on, dragging one end of the BBQ while the other pushed. The grill frame clunked over the platform's ridge as the doors closed. Then I watched my train draw away again.

I thanked Phil for thinking about me. But I was enjoying my life in London. I was busy and cheerful, and I hoped to assist Labour win from afar.

The chat didn't conclude right away. We debated briefly, with Phil arguing that there was never a good moment to run, but now was better than most, and me evading. While he didn't go into detail about why he was asking me, Phil praised him for picking up the phone and calling.

I had left politics in New Zealand, but I kept thinking about it. Did I have what it takes to run? Let alone tolerate the rigours of parliamentary life? No, I did not think so. But there was a voice in my head that I couldn't ignore. What if.

"Thank you for asking, Phil," I replied. "But no thank you."

Months have passed. The days got a little warmer. I stopped taking the train and began walking to work, listening to the news from home as I marched along the Thames. I could feel the election approaching—the tension, the excitement, and my absence. Although I was hundreds of kilometers away, I wished I could be there. I'd phone my friends to find out what I had missed and what was going on. Then one day, I had an idea to fill the void. Why not bring the campaign here?

I considered running a voter registration drive in London to encourage New Zealanders living here to vote. After all, all you had to do to be eligible to vote was visit New Zealand once in the previous three years. I could put together a team to help. It might even feel like a campaign back home, and even if it didn't, I'd feel like I was contributing.

Then, one morning, while I was in my new Brixton flat, I received another call, this one from Grant. Grant and I became good friends after sharing that small little office in the Beehive. We had discussed everything—work issues, my religious challenges, and what we would do after we left the Beehive.

He joked that we'd spent so much time together that he had corrupted me. He had a terrible potty mouth, and somewhere along the way, I started swearing sporadically in a way that my aunty Marie would have approved of. I was also with him after my first experience with drinking too much alcohol. The next morning, Grant asked what I had eaten. When I informed him I'd only eaten a few bits of porridge, he shook his head. "Come with me." We proceeded to the cafeteria, and he purchased me a greasy sausage bun with tomato sauce. It was medicinal.

By early 2008, Grant had also left the Beehive. He worked at University of Otago. But he'd decided to run as the Labour candidate in Wellington Central, a prominent district in the nation's capital. It would be a challenging race. But in my mind, there was never a question. The grant was made for Parliament.

On the phone, we talked briefly about my London voter registration drive. I was almost fanatical about it, recruiting volunteers and producing T-shirts and pull-up banners. We planned to attend rugby games, festivals, and other occasions where we knew New Zealanders would be present to ensure their enrollment. We even had a slogan: "Have your say from far away." What we lacked, however, was a hook, the kind of thing that could truly drive turnout and media attention.

"You know, Jacinda," Grant stated. "If you wanted to help Labour from over there, you could try to get a spot on the party list."

The party list. I began pacing around the lounge. Of course, the party list.

To appreciate what Grant was saying, you must first comprehend the New Zealand electoral system, sometimes known as mixed-member proportional (MMP). In MMP, each voter has two votes: electorate and party vote. The electorate vote is straightforward: you vote for the candidate you want to represent your local region in Parliament. The candidate who receives the most votes wins the seat. The majority of Parliament's seats—72 out of 120—are filled this manner.

Your party vote, on the other hand, allows you to vote for the political party you want to see form the government. Most of the time, voters cast their party vote for their chosen candidate's party. In New Plymouth, for example, this meant voting for Harry first, followed by Labour. On election night, all votes are counted. If a party receives a higher share of the party vote than the seats earned through electorate voting, they are eligible for a "top up"—some extra MPs picked from their party list—which Grant encouraged me to apply for.

The list included the whole roster of possible MPs, sorted in ascending order. Helen Clark, the Labour Party's leader, is ranked first on the list. The leader is followed by the heavy hitters, largely incumbent MPs, with a few promising newcomers thrown in between, all the way down to practically every candidate seeking for a seat and some who are not. Being on the list did not guarantee you would become an MP—there were more individuals on it than there were winnable seats—but it was an excellent way to help the party.

My voter enrollment effort required a platform. Perhaps if I could refer to myself as an actual candidate rather than simply some random guy attempting to register votes, I could garner more media coverage and more people voting.

It seemed Grant was reading my mind too. "Being on the list will probably help your enrollment drive," he stated into the phone. Even from this distance of nearly nineteen thousand kilometers, he knew how to persuade me of something.

And I could image him walking around his couch, adjusting his troubled back, and raising his brow playfully as he delivered the clincher.

"I think it could really help the party, Jacinda."

I held my breath for a few seconds, trying to determine if I was nervous or excited.

"Huh," I finally said. "Maybe I will."

Following that, everything progressed rapidly. I flew to Wellington for the regional list conference, when the local party list is compiled and ranked. It felt strange to be back, like if two years had barely passed. Mum and Dad followed me, and as we walked across the gravel parking lot, I explained what was about to happen. In some ways, it would be similar to speed dating. I and dozens of other candidates, including Grant, would present myself to small groups of local Labour members, field questions, and share our vision for the party. We'd all be ranked regionally, and in a few weeks, the national committee would combine all of the regional lists into one, with numerical ranks assigned to everyone.

My mother was cheery and encouraging, but my father was less certain. "Is it really a smart idea to run for something you're unlikely to win? " Dad inquired, frowning. I expressed my reasoning. That it could help with our campaign in London, and that raising our party's vote there was critical. Especially in tight races like Wellington Central, which Grant was running in.

We strolled into the musty hall, which was used for Boy Scout meetings. As I walked in, I nodded hello to recognizable faces—people I'd worked with on campaigns or with unions. Inside, stackable seats were arranged facing the front. I stood in the back of the room, searching the crowd until I spotted Grant. Technically, we were competitors. But Grant was the person I most wanted to see in Parliament. He was progressive, astute, witty, and kind. If Grant did not win his race, a high ranking on the list would be his ticket to Parliament. As far as I was concerned, today was Grant's.

When the time came, I moved between groups, cheerfully introducing myself and answering questions.

Hello, my name is Jacinda, and I am working on an enrollment drive in London.

Why am I here? I, too, have been a party member and campaign volunteer for many years. I want to help Labour win.

After the speed dating, we reunited as one large group to begin the ranking process. I sat with Mum and Dad and watched MPs be nominated.

Nominations. Seconder. Aye. Initially, it was merely a formality, ranking existing MPs. Then the first fresh opening appeared.

"Nominations? Silence fell over the room. A member of Grant's squad stood and cried, "Grant Robertson!" "I waited for the seconder to stand. Instead, Grant stood.

"I don't want to be ranked," Grant replied. "Not until Jacinda Ardern has been." He gave me a smirk that said, "I know exactly what I just did," before returning his gaze to the front. I sat motionless in the room, watching the entire process buzz around me. Someone nominated me, another seconded it, and I was included to the list. Grant had just promised that I'd be ranked higher than him. That conduct could mean the difference between him serving in Parliament and not. It remains one of the most selfless and gracious political deeds I have ever witnessed.

It also moved me closer to Parliament.

By the time the national committee met to combine all the regional lists into a final rating for each candidate, I had returned to my flat in London. It was 5:00 a.m. When my Nokia sprang to life.

"Mate," said a husky voice from the other end of the phone. My friend Tolley, the union head, had helped me schedule Helen Clark's campus visit, during which I had lost my cool.

"You're No. 20, mate. "You're number 20."

No. 20? That meant that the party had ranked me higher than the sitting MPs. I had worked hard in the party, established strong networks, and was as dedicated to seeing Labour elected as anyone else. But I was still astonished.

I sat upright in bed. My room was dark and quiet, while my flatmates slept in the rooms above me. In the last election, Labour won fifty seats. Labour has never won fewer than thirty-seven seats since the MMP system was implemented.

Whatever occurred on Election Day, I was almost certain to be elected to Parliament.

The booing did not start loudly. It started with a murmur, a quiet chord from a small group of people—the early adopters, if you will. At first, the noise appeared nearly ambient. Then others joined in. Then more. It quickly became a magnificent chorus of complete scorn.

I was at my first candidate meeting, and things were going poorly. Around fifty people had met in Matamata, twenty minutes outside Morrinsville, in a community room with a low ceiling and comfortable chairs. The moderator was from an agricultural organization called Federated Farmers, and the majority of the audience was conservative. Each time the National Party candidate spoke, the entire crowd nodded and their eyes lit up. Then it was my turn. The question concerned climate change. I don't remember the precise words, but I do recall the implication: Did I "believe" in it?

As soon as I started to respond, I noticed arms folding and heads shaking. Smiles turned into wary glares. My gaze flickered to the back of the room. My mother sat up straight in her chair and smiled at me, as if her warmth could compensate for everyone else's contempt. My grandmother Margaret sat next to her, her wide rectangular spectacles reflecting a certain doubt. The corners of her mouth turned downward in a displeasured expression.

My grandma had offered me her automobile a few weeks ago so that I could go door knocking. She had worn the same face as she watched Granddad Eric, who gently and carefully assisted me in mounting a set of speakers and Labour placards on the car top. When a neighbor passed by, Grandma Margaret cried out, "The things you do for your grandchildren!" "Let there be no doubt about her political affiliation.

My grandmother was no fan of Labor. However, unlike the other participants, she did not boo me as I answered the climate change question. I looked at her for one more beat. At least I didn't believe my grandmother was booing me.

I was deeply concerned about climate change. The Māori notion of kaitiakitanga, which holds that we are all protectors of the land, sea, and sky, felt very real to me. I could clearly recall studying as a child about the hole in the ozone layer and the dangers of chemicals found in aerosol cans. It had a particularly strong impact on our region's atmosphere, which meant that New Zealand received less sun protection than most other countries.

My childlike mind connected the dots. People around the world use hairspray. Should I wear extra sunscreen? It was the first time I realized that not only do humans have an impact on the environment, but so do our choices, even if we live hundreds of miles apart. Now, with the climate crisis, we are witnessing this dynamic on a grand scale. Climate change posed a threat to New Zealand's coastlines, low-lying areas, and Pacific neighbors.

Labour had recently approved a scheme for pricing carbon, but not without controversy. Rural areas such as Matamata were concerned that agricultural pollutants, particularly from cows burping, would be included in this program. Some thought this was unfair, while others refused to think methane was a problem at all. A couple had even taken their tractors to the Beehive to make their point, with one National Party MP driving a rusted, muddy Massey Ferguson tractor up the steps of Parliament. Shane Ardern was my distant cousin (by marriage, as Aunty Marie often reminded me).

But I think we needed to be open about what addressing climate change would entail. Even if it meant a wave of pain spreading across the room in the form of extremely vocal booing.

After the event—after the tepid applause, after I had shaken hands with my opponents, and after a fuming older man with black strands of hair combed over his bald head poked a finger in my face and called me a communist—I approached my mother and grandmother. Mum smiled encouragingly and rubbed my shoulder.

"Well done!" ", my mother said.

"Thank you, Mum. But I'm not sure it went well.

"Why did you think it was bad? "She inquired as if we were in two completely separate rooms.

"Ahh, the booing?" "I said.

She waved her hands dismissively. "I wouldn't worry about that."

I turned to face Grandma Margaret. "What did you think, Grandma?"

She craned her neck to look around the room. "I thought the candidate for New Zealand First was wonderful," she told me. She was referring to Barbara Stewart, a woman in her fifties who wore a huge black-and-white rosette pinned to her chest. She turned and looked at me with hope. Can you introduce me to her? "

That is when I realized. Even my granny may not vote for me.

I was not going to win the electorate vote. That was nearly likely, given that the electorate of Morrinsville was far too conservative for any Labour candidate.

But that didn't stop me from campaigning like the election depended on it.

I used every door-knocking method I learned in New Plymouth, rattling gates and knocking on doors in places where I knew there were Labour voters not once, but numerous times. I filled out endless enrollment forms alongside first-time voters and drove to the most remote regions of the district, where there were no volunteers to hand-deliver flyers.

And after four weeks, Election Day arrived. Labour had been lagging in all recent polls. The thought of winning seemed increasingly unlikely. But you wouldn't have known that from my aunty Marie's fierce campaigning in the last few days.

On election night, I wore a scarlet dress that I had purchased a few weeks before and black Mary Jane heels. My mother, Marie, and I got into Mum's new Toyota Corolla and drove to the Taniwharau League Club in Huntly, a large facility with a bar in the back and Labour posters leaning on the wall. We sat at a small round table, watching the results come in on a giant screen that typically showed rugby league games. I felt really overdressed among the patrons in track pants and rugby league shirts.

When my statistics came up, they merely reinforced what we all suspected. I had not won the rural conservative seat where I had grown up; I would have to rely on the party list. There was one bright spot that evening: Grant had won Wellington Central.

But the night's frustrations hadn't ended yet. Before long, Harry's results showed he had lost the New Plymouth seat by 105 votes. Marie sobbed beside me. That's when we departed.

We were driving home in the dark, Mum dozing beside me and Marie sobbing in the backseat, when Helen Clark arrived at the Labour Party's election night headquarters, acknowledged defeat to John Key, and resigned.

Labour had lost the government. The conservative National Party would be in control. I reflected on everything that Labour had accomplished and all that could be undone.

But Labour had received 34% of the party vote, more than enough to guarantee me a seat in Parliament. I intended to become a Parliament member.

When you are sworn in to Parliament, the event may be bittersweet. Maybe you're in opposition, watching another party seize control of the government. MPs you admired, or perhaps worked for, may no longer be present, with the formal nameplates on their doors gone and replaced with new names. All of the things you intended to do and change will have to wait—when is unclear.

And yet, one November morning, you wake up early. You put on a black jacket and gently clip a gold-plated bracelet with a bamboo design onto your wrist. A few hours later, you'll cross the barrier from the "ayes or noes" lobby into the debate room, which has high ceilings, wood panels, and green leather chairs. Sit in one of those chairs. And

when your name is called, you walk the debating chamber floor, raise your hand, and are sworn in, you will still be happy.
It could even feel like an honor of a lifetime.

CHAPTER 10

I knew I was late before I looked at my watch. I had taken the incorrect path inside Parliament House. Now I was standing at one end of a big hallway with red carpet and cream walls. Was I even on the correct floor?

I'd been an MP for less than a week. Like the other new MPs, I was part of an orientation session and received a large white binder full of colorful tabs and instructions on how to set up my offices, access the Parliament library, and fill out mileage logbooks. The curriculum also included in-person workshops, such as today's practice run in the debating chamber to ensure we understood how to utilize the microphones. That's where I was going now. All thirty or so new MPs would be there, training as if it were the first day of a high school debate camp.

When I arrived at the chamber's entrance, the session had already begun. Newly elected representatives sat on green leather chairs, with wooden desks set in front of them and black microphones protruding from the top. A figure in a black robe stepped in front of them, most likely from the clerk's office, but I can't remember who it was or what they were saying. I just recall crouching down as I passed, like if I had arrived late to a movie theater and was looking for an available seat near the first row.

I dropped my folder on the bench and sat in the silky leather chair, slipping a little further than I expected. I stood up and gazed in the faces around me. That was the moment. That's when I realized I was an MP. I was seated in the debating chamber, not for a tour or a ceremony, but because it was now my responsibility to be there.

While the debate chamber may appear majestic, it may also feel like a battle ring. First, there's the tiered seating and horseshoe configuration: government MPs on one side and opposition on the other, with members of the public staring down from the viewing area above, much like gladiatorial spectators. That is precisely how it might seem during the blood sport of question time.

It wasn't like when I was booed while campaigning in Matamata. After all, booing is a generic type of noise that can be ignored due to its lack of specificity. This was different. I was being jeered loudly and audibly, and the words were painfully clear.

For a minute, I stood there, taking everything in. We all appeared like adults, dressed in formal clothing and taking themselves very seriously. But you could just as well place us in a schoolyard and say we were arguing about a game of handball. One of the MPs appeared very happy. She was a very intelligent woman, self-assured and well-respected by all. She wore stylish clothing and spoke with the accent of someone who had attended private school. But here she was, hair bouncing back and forth, heated face, waving her finger at me as if we were just two kids in the school corridor. As the insults grew louder, people of my own party began to yell in my defense.

I don't want to listen!

Can't stand hearing a good argument!

I didn't know Trevor, but I'd seen him while working for Helen Clark's office, typically when he was in difficulty. In those days, Labour MPs who stepped out of line, spoke out of turn, or breached a rule could expect to hear from Heather, sometimes known as H2. Trevor frequently heard from H2. He had served in Parliament for decades, long enough to have fought to decriminalize homosexuality in 1986. He had the physique of a high school rugby coach and was aggressive, impulsive, and blunt—a partisan attack dog who enraged his opponents and occasionally irritated his allies. During an impassioned debate in the chamber, one of the opposing members made a nasty remark about Trevor's family. Trevor motioned for the MP to "come outside" at the end of the session and slapped him after a heated verbal exchange in the foyer.

A few days after my gaffe in the debating chamber, I chased Trevor down the hallway. I detailed my most recent error, then stated plainly, "I need to toughen up." I told him that if I didn't stop caring about what others said to and about me, this job would be too difficult. And, being the roughest and least empathetic person I knew, could he help me?

Trevor paused walking and turned to face me. As he listened, his countenance expressed surprise, and he furrowed his brow. "Jacinda, is that how you see me?"

Was he joking? That is how everyone saw him. I grinned, figuring it was apparent.

Trevor averted his gaze briefly. Then he leaned in. In a quiet, clear voice, he urged, "Promise me you will not try to toughen up, Jacinda. You experience emotions because you have empathy and care. The instant you alter, you'll lose your edge at work." Trevor offered me a comforting look and marched down the hallway.

In opposition, there were few ways to change anything. We could create laws for the biscuit tin and hope our number gets called. We may propose modifications to bills or clarify new laws, but these were rarely effective. But the major influence we had was to raise public opposition to the government's agenda—which wasn't much. Every time I phoned my sister, I was reminded of how irrelevant we were. I'd explain massive political debates over subjects I thought were critical to our country's future, only to hear her say, "Oh, I missed all that." Louise, like many others, saw the party's back-and-forth as mere "politics."

A few weeks after joining Parliament, I received a call from the producer of the country's largest morning show. Breakfast was New Zealand's equivalent of Good Morning America or the Today show, with hours-long chat shows transmitted live to hundreds of thousands of households across the country. It featured a weekly program called "Young Guns," in which two young backbench MPs, one from National and one from Labour, debated current problems. The producer informed me that he intended to do a trial with me and Simon Bridges, an upcoming National Party MP.

I liked Simon. He was a new MP, like myself, and had become active in politics as a teenager. Simon was the youngest of six children, the son of a Baptist preacher, and he exuded easy, genial confidence and a self-deprecating sense of humor. While this was simply a test run, if Simon and I performed well—if we could communicate properly and

New Zealand loved us—we might continue. If not, they would try someone else. Initially, it felt more like Survivor than a morning chat program.

That did not mean I enjoyed being on television. I've always felt uneasy and self-conscious. I grinned through it, however. I laughed, exchanged ideas, and constructed political arguments. But inside, I was constantly multitasking. Thinking about the last thing I said while deciding what to say next.

But that assumed everyone was interested in what we were saying.

One day, a press secretary said, "Everyone watches with the sound turned down, you know." I wasn't sure if it was intended to help me feel better about any potential faults or to have me concentrate more on how I appeared. As it was, I had to appear to the Breakfast studio 20 minutes before Simon to get my makeup done. And I am sure I spent more time worrying what I would wear. In fact, the longer I did the section, the more self-conscious I felt. Perhaps it was because of the person who paid fifty cents for a postage stamp merely to mail me a cut from a pet food advertisement displaying a cartoon of a dog with a huge set of fangs. Above it, in all-caps ballpoint lettering, were the words "WHY DO YOU LOOK LIKE THIS?" Other criticisms were marginally more courteous. Like the email I received from a Breakfast watcher who was certain that my coppery hair clashed with Simon's black hair. Had I considered dying mine?

Women in public glare experience another reality. It is completely different for women. Every time I turned on the television, I felt this intensely. Perhaps this is why, when I received a call from the editor of a women's magazine asking if I would participate in a series on body image, a piece to empower women, I said yes. This was an opportunity to discuss how it felt to continuously see yourself through the eyes of others, comparing yourself to some unsaid, unreachable standard. We can be ourselves without revealing too much. Be comfortable, but not dowdy. Dress smartly but not overly fancy. Being in the public eye had made me more self-conscious, but it had also strengthened my conviction that the added scrutiny women experienced was unjust. So, the response was yes; I would be delighted to discuss body image with ladies all throughout New Zealand.

Sometimes we were able to put a halt to things we disagreed with, such as the government's proposal to mine in protected zones. Or we could design bills for the biscuit tin, such as my child poverty bill. Sometimes those bills were brought forth, such as the one I wrote to reform adoption laws. And every day, as an MP, I met people I could help.

Early on, I met a grandma who was parenting her grandchild with shaken infant syndrome. Music therapy was beneficial, but the government had reduced her money for it. I helped get it reestablished. Then there was the business owner, who explained that due to a peculiarity in New Zealand law, when they placed a New Zealand censorship rating to a DVD or CD, they had to do so behind the clear wrapper rather than on top of it. This required additional time and money to reseal the packages. I was able to modify the law and repair it. It was modest and bureaucratic, but it benefitted someone.

There was always something you could do to help people, and the small things added up to a sense of usefulness. And, more often than not, that was enough to propel you forward, to keep you going even on the most difficult days.

Nikki and I were the same age and had comparable backgrounds. Like me, she became active in politics at a young age. She had previously lived in London, as had I. The duel between two young women in opposing parties was promptly called by one journalist "the Battle of the Babes." We were seen as a curiosity, but also as two young women in politics, which made us interchangeable.

I worked hard during that election campaign. I bought a tiny eight-foot caravan, painted it Labour colors, and took it to festivals and street corners to conduct pop-up events. I discovered ways to go inside apartment buildings and knock on the doors of otherwise inaccessible voters. I put up posters across the city, distributed flyers, and held public meetings. I organized a large group of volunteers who became like family. Among them was Barbara Ward, an active and quietly

brilliant woman who knew Auckland Central like the back of her hand and went on to work in my office there, where she still works today.
I gave it all. Nonetheless, Nikki retained her Auckland seat by 717 votes on election night in 2011, and Labour lost to National once more. While Phil, the Labour leader, had gained enough party votes to ensure that list MPs like me could continue to serve in Parliament, I knew he would step down as leader. Everything else remained undetermined.
I was devastated as I walked away from our election night event with a few volunteers down Ponsonby Road, a prominent stretch of affluent pubs and restaurants highlighted by design businesses. I wore a bright red cowl-neck dress and the same Mary Janes that I had worn on election night three years ago. It was late, and revelers streamed out onto the streets, carrying on with their lives while we felt oppressed. I passed a bunch of young individuals leaving one of the clubs near a burger bar. A young woman locked eyes with me. "Hey," she exclaimed. "Nice dress!"
I thanked her. "I'll take it," I thought.
She craned her neck backward and said, "But those shoes make your ankles look fat!"
My second term, even as a list MP, was busier than the first. I became the social development spokesman, dealing with issues ranging from the assistance system to child protection. I kept performing "Young Guns" and other media, doing my best to boost Labour's visibility. And I attended numerous events, including gallery openings, award shows, and community activities. One seasoned member of our team once warned me, "Never eat while standing up," referring to the consequences of an infinite supply of canapés. But it was the persistent requirement for a plus-one that I found difficult. More often than not, Barbara Ward sacrificed countless evenings of her life to ensure I was never alone at an event.
We attended school quiz evenings and local fundraisers. I even agreed to DJ at a small record store called Real Groovy. For an hour, I stood near the front of the store, playing Janis Joplin mixed with the Unknown Mortal Orchestra. Following that, I was requested to

perform at a music event called Laneway, and "DJ" was incorrectly put to my list of vocations.

In October 2012, I attended the Restaurant of the Year Awards in Auckland with another friend, Colin. He was a model, a television host, and a good companion. Metro magazine hosted the dinner, and Colin was one of two cover stars in the restaurant issue. It was an extraordinarily luxurious night, with celebrities in attendance, held in a key city church with the seats removed and replaced by long tables and dark lighting.

By this stage, I was used to attending events and galas. I was used to making small conversation. I wasn't used to seeing prominent individuals. So, when Colin introduced us all, I felt like a nerdy debate student. But I also observed Clarke's gaze darting about the room. He was gorgeous, like everyone else around me, with a strong jaw, dark eyes, and slightly disheveled dark hair, but he didn't appear to be at ease in either the environment or his complete suit. Huh, I thought, astonished by his awkwardness. I guess I've done enough of these to pretend I belong here.

Two years into my second period, I flew to London to see my sister who was having a baby. She had been with her partner, Ray, for some years. They met salsa dancing and now lived together in a little flat on the outskirts of town. This would be Louise's first child and my first niece.

My sister's delivery experience was not easy. I knew this, but when I arrived at the hospital, she hardly had the energy to meet me. She was pale, had a blood transfusion, and her hair was matted across her forehead. She tried to sit upright. Baby Isabella lay near the base of the bed. My mother lingered nearby and fussed about.

I bent over the Perspex bassinet and noticed Isabella's little pixie ears. They looked exactly like my sister's. Unlike Louise, her eyes were black, as was the hair that adorned her tiny head. I felt an instant connection to this tiny human. Like she's part of me.

While I was caught up in the maelstrom of politics, Louise was forging her own path, using her intelligence and science degree to work in quality control for a pharmaceutical company. And now she was a mother, too. I admired Isabella's small face and beautiful features and wondered whether she was the only child I'd ever have the opportunity to feel that way about.

I was thirty-three. I worked ceaselessly. Since entering Parliament, the longest relationship I'd had was three months. Perhaps, unknowingly, I had already prioritized politics over family. Nonetheless, I had made no decision. I was still thinking about parenting all the time. My desire to become a mother was not a "desire" at all; it was an assumption. A given.

I felt as if a small part of myself had been allocated as the space for mothering, and that one day I'd be able to enjoy that area on an actual child. I may have left the religion, but none of those preconceptions had left me. I still felt that I was meant to get educated, marry and have children in that order.

I'm not sure if my family still thought that was where I was going. My mother had long believed that my life would follow a more traditional path, even after I left the church. After my sister's wedding, many years ago, my mother casually stated, "Jacinda, we spent $4,000 on Louise's wedding, so I have put the same amount aside for you when you get married." She said this not to add pressure, but to preserve it on record. My mother, after all, came from a family of five children, so she was fiercely committed to fairness.

I hadn't given my wedding budget much attention until I moved to London and my mother contacted. "You know that money I put aside for your wedding," she told me. "Well, I've decided to put it in long-term investment bonds." Nothing screams "I think you'll be single for a while" like that.

Then, when I was first elected to Parliament and required a car, Mum dealt the ultimate blow. "How about instead of giving you that wedding money, I just give you my Toyota Corolla?" My dowry was now a red 1996 Toyota Corolla hatchback.

During my visit to see my niece, I sat on the floor of my sister's modest lounge in her London flat and opened my laptop. My sister was now home, resting while Isabella slept. My mother was across the room, folding the wash. I'd be returning to New Zealand in just a few days. I opened my inbox and found a flurry of work-related texts. But there was one email I did not expect.

"Huh," I replied.

Across the room, my mother looked up from folding towels. "What is it?"

My eyes examined the message. "Just an email from a guy who works in radio back home." It had been over a year since I first met Clarke Gayford at the restaurant awards, and I didn't believe he would remember.

"Apparently, he is dissatisfied with the government." He claims he'd like to help with my campaign.

"Well, that's nice," my mother responded, picking up another towel.

"Yeah," I responded, tapping the reply button. "It is nice."

CHAPTER 11

After losing the election, Phil Goff resigned. When David Shearer discovered he didn't have the support of his colleagues, he, too, left. David Cunliffe made a different decision.

Cunliffe convened a meeting of the Labour team, including those who had lost seats in Parliament, a few days after the election. I've been to a lot of meetings in my time, and this remains one of the worst. While there is always a deflated drab flatness in the days following a loss, the overall atmosphere after the 2014 election was darker than typical. We gathered in a tiny ground-floor meeting room just large enough for our depleted staff. We'd been using this area for a while, ever since David opted to repurpose the traditional caucus room as his own "war room," bringing his advisers from more private offices into an open-plan style so they could function as "one seamless machine."

David sat in the front of the room, behind a table, while we faced him from chairs arranged in rows. He gave some preliminary remarks before opening the floor. According to tradition, what happens in a caucus room stays in the caucus room. I will always follow this rule. But what happened next was exactly what you'd expect if you left a pot on the burner and kept increasing the heat without releasing it. The lid eventually blows off.

Some persons in that room had lost their jobs, while others had lost hope. Many had lost both. But it wasn't just that. There were MPs from electorates where people faced the most extreme, degrading poverty. These MPs recognized precisely what our loss meant. So, one by one, they stood up, some in tears, some angry, and said exactly that. I remember seeing two brand-new MPs. They'd been silent, like possums in headlights, their eyes flickering from speaker to speaker as they took in all of the wrath and misery. Their expressions appeared to imply, "Are caucus meetings always like this?"

Hours have passed. Finally, Trevor Mallard rose. "Look," he said. "Can I make a proposal before we go on? "

We awaited his pearl of wisdom. "Can I suggest"—he asked, then paused again, gazing around at all of us before finishing—"that we take a break to buy a couple sausage rolls? "

I learned two things that day. First, never let a team sit in frustration. Second, always consider snacks.

A week later, David resigned, resulting in a new leadership campaign, which he soon announced he would run in. I can't tell you David's reasoning behind this decision—it never made sense to me—but I'm guessing he believed he had the backing of Labour members and wanted to prove it with a party contest. To make his statement, he went to Auckland, where the Labour Party's national council was convening at a trade union headquarters. However, because the union had not yet approved a candidate for party head, David was ordered to make his statement outside the premises. David went a few hundred meters down the road in Kingsland's busy streets, unwittingly making his statement outside a brothel. Every street corner in politics presents a horrible photo opportunity.

Other leadership contenders, including Grant, David Parker, Nanaia Mahuta, and Andrew Little, also raised their hands. Andrew was a former union leader and lawyer, so when he declared his candidacy, it was assumed that he would garner union support. Andrew's participation into the campaign was the final straw for David Cunliffe, who pulled out of the competition forever. I felt relieved for the first time in awhile.

I liked and respected all the leadership candidates, but Grant remained my top choice. Instead of having me join his campaign, he invited me to run as his deputy. I was hesitant to take on the job, but Grant persuaded that running as a team would generate more votes. I wanted him to win, so we made a ticket, or, as a caricature that merged our two faces described us, Gracinda.

Our campaign launch took place at a neighborhood bar in Auckland that overlooked the city. Grant had had his hair cut for the occasion, and in his well-fitted suit and scarlet tie, he appeared fresh and, he admits, uncharacteristically polished. I put on bright lipstick and wore

a light-colored jacket with a silver glitter, hoping that would compensate for the fact that I was quite ill. The day before, I awoke with my throat on fire. Clarke had taken me to see the doctor, who had shrugged unhelpfully.
"Probably viral; nothing we can do. "Try slugging back some brandy."
I had done that, and consumed large amounts of vitamin C. It had not helped.
Grant noticed I was unwell the moment I arrived. "You sound terrible," he replied quietly, aware of the media presence.
"Thanks," I murmured, doing my best to grin for the cameras. A few minutes later, fueled by excitement, I presented Grant with the most impassioned speech I could muster. Clarke found me at home many hours later, on the couch, still dressed in my launch outfit and barely able to speak. He placed down the soup he'd brought me and motioned toward the door.
"Come on," he replied. "I'm taking you to the emergency room."
I was hospitalized with a secondary infection from tonsillitis known as quinsy. It hit me hard, and I was in and out of the hospital twice. During my second hospitalization, a right-wing figure said I was experiencing a mental breakdown.
Lying in my hospital bed, an open cut in my mouth, unable to eat or speak, I considered what to do. It was another of those lose-lose decisions that come with politics. If I addressed the rumor publicly, even to reject it, I risked propagating the deception. I hadn't even heard of that rumor till she denied it, as one would say. Worse, replying to a rumor may have the unintended consequence of legitimizing it: if it was significant enough for her to respond, perhaps it is true?
Then there was the rumor's substance. What if my throat hadn't been the cause of my hospitalization? I despised the concept of someone's mental health being weaponized in this way. But, of course, these rumors had a purpose. The person who made the claim was attempting to portray me as "unstable," too "fragile" to be a deputy, and possibly even in politics. They had apparently said as much. The most strategic response seems to be to simply continue.

I was out of commission for two weeks, and when I recovered, I devoted my entire effort to Grant's campaign for party leadership. Grant was so close, I could feel it. He and I attended campaign meetings, worked the phones, sent several emails, and had open chats with party members in which I conveyed what I knew about Grant as a person. Not only did I believe in his principles, but also his leadership style. He demonstrated empathy, respect, and principle. The conversations were generally favorable. But not all.

In Grant's prior leadership campaigns, there had been whispers about his sexuality. Those questions loomed larger this time, perhaps because he was closer than ever before. Some media commented publicly about whether New Zealand is ready for a gay leader.

I was walking near my home when a top party member called to discuss the race. I knew this man well. He loved Grant and respected him, so hearing him remark, "New Zealand won't vote for him" startled me. I was walking steeply at the time, and I couldn't tell if my huffing was due to the elevation or my outraged fury.

"Why should we pass that judgment on behalf of the people of New Zealand? "I asked. I believed that voters deserved far more credit than this individual was giving them, and how could we ever test that if we, as a progressive party, were unwilling to even have a gay candidate?

I knew Grant was concerned about the impact of any harsh and insulting discussions regarding his sexuality. "I worry," Grant told me privately, "about the young people watching." This was his recurring refrain. After all, he was one of those youngsters.

Around this time, I was walking down K Road, the equivalent of a red-light district, to participate in a Pride debate, a fundraiser for a young rainbow organization. That was when I heard someone say my name. The voice was unknown, but something about its tone suggested it was someone I knew.

I turned around to see the person standing in front of me dressed from head to toe in a figure-hugging gold dress, towering platforms, and an enormous beehive hairdo topped with glittering makeup and crimson lipstick. A gorgeous and confident drag queen. They were beautiful. But, did I know them?

Apparently I did. "Jacinda, it's me," they said. There was something about their posture, the gentleness of their expression. Some profound memories began to emerge. Maybe I knew them.

"It's me," they added. "It's Walter."

It was suddenly so evident. Walter, my beloved Mormon friend from Murupara. The sweet child who had collected scent cards years before and had played the wolf in our church's rendition of Little Red Riding Hood. Walter, who joined me in dressing up as Smurfs for school but was so eager to be Smurfette that we traded, so I went to school that day as Papa Smurf. Of course. Walter. We laughed and hugged, and it felt like it hadn't been more than 25 years.

I wanted to ask so many questions, but time didn't allow. Instead, I left our brief meeting on K Road that day convinced that—whether you are born into a Mormon or an agnostic household, a little village like Murupara or a major city like Auckland—we are who we are, and no one should ever be told that is insufficient.

Not Grant. Not Walter. Not anyone.

Not ever.

We gathered in Wellington to hear the leadership announcement. After the ballots were tabulated, the party's president discreetly informed the candidates of the results. Then they all filed into a larger room with other MPs and reporters, anxious to hear who would finally lead us to victory.

I stood in the rear of the caucus chamber, with Clarke by my side. He had flown down to Wellington knowing that if Grant won, I would be the deputy leader. He wanted to be there "just in case." I wasn't sure if he meant to console or rejoice. It didn't really matter. I was simply grateful to have him there.

I rocked back and forth on my heels. Hoping. Willing. Grant may have represented a new generation of leaders. But he wasn't about to keep trying and failing. He had made it clear during the campaign—this was his final attempt—that if he did not win the leadership this time, it meant the party did not want him.

When the door opened, I examined Grant. His head was down, watching where he put each foot. As soon as he entered the caucus room, he raised his head and locked eyes with me. And I knew. He sported an awkward, almost forced smile. I'd read his smile a thousand times before. This time, it read, "We tried."

Moments later, it was announced that Andrew Little had been named the next Labour leader. Grant had lost one percent.

I couldn't express any feeling. It would have been unfair. Andrew, our new leader, was also my colleague. I liked him too. But Grant's loss felt immense. From the minute we started working together, I saw Grant as someone who could transform the way we looked at politicians, and possibly even change who aspired to be one. But now it was gone. And for good.

He could have been terrific, I reasoned. And now we will never know. Andrew Little exuded sincerity, which I admired. Before leading the party, he served as national secretary of the Engineers Union. He worked tirelessly and exhibited fervor in the debate chamber, earning him the nickname Angry Andy. It felt unjust to me. What I saw was someone ready to battle.

We had spent six years in opposition and had learned a few lessons. Andrew brought a new level of discipline to our squad. All the leaks that had destabilized the party for so many years had subsided. We worked hard to develop electoral policies and articulate our vision. We were, I thought, beginning to appear ready to govern.

I got along well with Andrew. I always had. He granted me a place on his front bench and handed me the justice portfolio, and the arts, small business, and children's policies. I continued to promote Best Start, the child tax credit, and the child poverty statutes that I had developed. I wanted to understand what was going on in state care, so I reviewed years' worth of coroners' reports for children who had died while supposed to be protected by government agencies, spoke with specialists, and tried to figure out where the system was failing children. Nonetheless, a constant refrain began to emerge about me. It primarily came from pundits, who made purposeful jabs in articles or opinion pieces. What did she do? They stated I had made "no important contribution in [my] portfolio work" and that "pretty faces get you only so far." I was dubbed insipid, vacuous, and even "pretty bloody stupid." The criticism was so pervasive that I found myself repeating it in my own brain. What did I do?

I had worked hard for three terms to create ideas that were ready for implementation. But I had shot them into the air like a flare gun, expecting them to attract everyone's attention or make an impact. They had not. In a never-ending media cycle, policy statements or striking an agreement did not pique editors' interest or generate a catchy headline. Right or wrong, the media required a boxing ring with politicians at each corner. That was their passport to success, and by extension, ours. However, as far as I could tell, this strategy was not without consequences.

I had been visiting schools regularly. If I needed to clear my mind, I went to a school. If I was anxious, running low on energy, or in need of inspiration, I'd go to school. I enjoyed discussing politics and decision-making with young people, and I appreciated the incisive questions they offered. During these visits, I would frequently discuss leadership with the students and put their beliefs to the test. I'd ask students to close their eyes, visualize a politician, and describe what they saw. They'd raise their hands and describe the visuals that came to mind—"male," "old," "gray." Then they'd focus on what they heard or the tone of voice of this imaginary person. The words would appear rapidly. "Confident." "Angry." "Aggressive." I repeated this practice in schools across the country, and the results were always the same. And it's no wonder students believed it based on what they saw in the media.

I'd never be that type of leader, and I didn't want to try. If the only way to score runs against the opposition was to attack and tear people down, I might have been mediocre. I did not want to have to pick between being a good politician and a good person. So I settled into the criticism.

But, even after I'd accepted that, I was confronted with a new issue: media conjecture about something I never expected to have to deal with publicly—whether or not I was pregnant.

CHAPTER 12

We were in the middle of another election year, 2017, when I found myself with the flu. I'd been in bed for days feeling weak and sorry for myself. I had been drifting in and out of sleep when I grabbed my phone. What time is it anyway? Ten thirty in the morning. That's when the text came. A journalist.

Are you free?

I drummed out a quick reply. I am sick.

A beat, then her response. How sick?

I told her it was the in-bed-for-days kind of sick, then added, Man flu. What's up? I didn't actually want to know what was up. I longed to close my eyes again, allow sleep to push away the pain in my head. But I worried if I didn't text her now, she'd call me.

The bosses have just heard the rumor about your bun, she wrote. I am confirming, as ordered, that you are Still Not Pregnant.

Ah. This again.

The rumors had been there for at least a month, maybe more. It started in May, the night of the government's budget announcement, which is one of the longest and most intense days in Parliament. The government releases its official budget for the year ahead; then the party in opposition does a deep dive into the numbers.

At the end of that day, a handful of MPs and staff had gone to the Beehive's bar for a drink. There, instead of getting a glass of wine, I'd opted for a soda and lime. When you are a woman of childbearing age in the spotlight, that's apparently all it takes. The questions started coming. One, then another. Then still more. Eventually, I'd gone on the record: No, I was not pregnant. But clearly my statement hadn't done the trick, because three weeks later here we were.

Feverish and irritated now, I drummed out a response to the reporter. I have many moments where I have real empathy for the job you do, and this is one of them. Confirming that I am still not pregnant and there is no reason to report on my reproductive organs. If they want breaking news, though, this man flu is a real ass.

I rolled over. Now I didn't just feel sick, I also felt sad. What I just told her was true. I wasn't pregnant. But I was trying.

It had been a whirlwind six months.

Last summer, things seemed pretty simple. Clarke and I began looking for a house together—a fixer-upper on a quiet little street in Auckland. We also began to talk about having kids.

But in early December, there was an unexpected vacancy in the Labour seat of Mount Albert, Helen Clark's old seat. The vacancy meant that there'd be a by-election, for this electorate only, even though the national election was still a year away. Mount Albert was a Labour stronghold, a mix of younger professionals, longtime residents, and a number of migrant families. It was also a chance to stop being reliant only on the party list and have a constituency of my own. I decided to run.

Soon after, Clarke and I closed on a home in Mount Albert, a cozy thirty-year-old one-story "brick and tile," New Zealand's equivalent of a bungalow, which we bought from an elderly widow. The house had peach carpeting and textured wallpaper, which we immediately began removing. Clarke was competent with almost any DIY project (except for the time a shower door shattered on his head). I, though, relied on the help of my mother to remove wallpaper, sand, and paint while juggling a campaign.

In February, I won the by-election for the Mount Albert district in what the media called a "landslide." While this was officially true—I won with 77 percent of the vote—the race wasn't exactly a nail-biter. The National Party didn't even run a candidate. The contest included me, a Green candidate, and an eclectic group of candidates from much smaller parties—among them the Communist League, the Legalise Cannabis Party, and Not a Party, whose entire platform consisted of encouraging people to boycott the election altogether. They got nineteen votes.

Still, I campaigned once again as if it were the race of my life. The only way I know how to campaign. And when it was over, I was, at last, an electorate MP with my very own constituency.

Not that there was any time to celebrate. It was still an election year. Voters would go to the polls in just seven months and this time, we felt hopeful.

Prime Minister John Key had recently announced his resignation. Often described as a compassionate conservative, he'd been prime minister for eight years. He'd managed to maintain solid levels of popularity throughout his time in office, even while doing unpopular things like increasing the goods and service tax and selling state assets. For us in Labour, his announcement created a great jolt of hope. It felt as if we'd been in the wilderness, these three long terms in opposition. Now that John Key was stepping down, there was an opening, an opportunity, and we wanted to take it.

But with the looming election came public commentary about a potential leadership shakeup in Labour—not at the party leader level, but at the No. 2 spot, the deputy leader to Andrew Little.

The current deputy leader was Annette King, my friend and the closest thing I had to a mentor. Annette had been in Parliament for over thirty years and had been a minister in multiple areas. She was pragmatic and wise, a sharp and effective politician who had helped stabilize the party during some of our rockiest moments.

Annette was also a master of compartmentalizing. Once, I saw her have a scorching exchange on the debating floor, the sort of thing that I'd have ruminated on for hours. The instant she sat back down in her chair, though, she picked up her phone, opened Candy Crush, and began calmly matching bright cartoon confections as if nothing had happened.

Annette looked after me; she also cheered me on, finishing conversations with you're doing great. Or after a long day, she might text me, saying, Well done today. She'd also repeatedly advised me to take charge of my schedule so politics didn't consume every part of my life. And because she probably didn't trust that I'd follow her advice, she'd even tried to set me up on a few dates, back before I met Clarke.

But a party's deputy leader is there, in part, to round out the ticket. Annette had done an incredible job as deputy leader. But some commentators suggested it might help the party to have a new face as second-in-command. Even Annette herself privately asked this question of Andrew. He'd said he wanted her to stay, but it didn't stop the questions from swirling.

While Annette and I might have seen each other as friends and collaborators, that was not how we were portrayed and I hated that. Whenever commentators discussed a possible leadership change, it was always presented simplistically: old versus new, last generation versus next generation. One cartoon depicted us as a mare and filly running side by side. Another showed Annette looking into a mirror with the words LABOUR DEPUTY inscribed above, and my toothy smile glaring back at her. There was never any nuance, no recognition that it wasn't a fight and that Annette and I were not at war with each other.

But amid all the speculation, Annette, in her signature style, decided to take the matter into her own hands. On March 1, she announced she would step down—not only as deputy leader, but also as an MP. She'd had thirty-three years in Parliament, eleven electoral cycles. She was ready to leave. And with that, Andrew asked me to take the deputy role.

On the evening Annette announced her plans, she texted me. You will be great, she wrote. Don't doubt yourself. Chin out and tell them you are ready.

Maybe I could tell them I was ready, but I didn't always feel ready. And the recent commentary when I took over the role of deputy didn't help. A senior journalist wrote in The New Zealand Herald on March 3, 2017, "So, Andrew Little has landed himself a show pony in Jacinda Ardern."

Oh. This again. Soon after Andrew announced I would be his deputy, I was seated in Copperfield's, when I heard a familiar voice coming from the debating chamber live stream. It was one of the government MPs, a young woman who was my age. She was standing on the debating chamber floor, giving a speech that included talking about my promotion. I saw the subtitles scroll across the screen, including my name, and the words "superficial cosmetic facelift." She went on, saying I'd been put in place only for the photo ops.

I was asked to respond to this commentary, as if responding weren't the same old catch-22. So, I said very little, throwing myself instead into the role and using my first official speech as deputy to talk about mental health for young people and the things that kept me in politics. Inside, though, I began to notice that something had changed when I heard comments like this. After eight years in Parliament, their shock had faded. They no longer surprised me; they no longer even offended me. In fact, something stronger was starting to happen. Hearing others insult me had begun to act as antidote to my impostor syndrome. Did I still doubt myself? Absolutely. But my own doubt was one thing. Hearing it publicly from others was something else entirely. I could feel how wrong their words were, in a way I'd never been able to when the doubts came from within me. I wasn't facile; I wasn't empty. And now I was determined to prove it.

Everything moved quickly in 2017. I had a new home, a new seat in Auckland, a new role in the party, and a new election on the horizon in a couple of months. And as if all of that weren't enough, I also had a new doctor—a fertility specialist.

I was thirty-six years old at that point, and realistic. When I didn't get pregnant after several months, I assumed my age was part of the issue and went to see a doctor for some tests.

I left a front bench meeting to take the call where my results were presented. They showed that I was unlikely to get pregnant without intervention. I tried to take in this news in the same way someone might take in news of a renovation project going wrong. As if it could just be "fixed," even though I knew better.

"Everything will be fine," Clarke assured me when I told him my test results. "We just need to be patient." He wasn't keen that we throw ourselves into any kind of treatment.

"I'm getting old," I told him. "This stuff doesn't get easier."

What I was really telling him was that I wanted to take some control over something that otherwise felt so out of my hands. I was scared that waiting would eventually mean never. So, a new phase began for us, one that required countless injections, many blood tests, and yo-yoing between labs and clinics.

Fertility treatments are a lot of work. It's not something you can slot into whatever space is available in your calendar. They take time, planning, and coordination. Trying to schedule it all while being an MP felt impossible. Sometimes I was in the wrong city when I needed blood work done. Other times I'd have to do consults remotely. On many of my plane trips, I toted a green cooler filled with injectable hormones, making me look as if I were carrying an organ for transplant.

At my lab visits for the near-constant blood tests, I'd sit in waiting rooms with my yellow fertility forms, noticing all of the other women holding the same yellow forms. I had joined an unspoken community united by a simple desire to have kids—a desire that I had taken for granted. And now there we all were. It was comforting and heartbreaking to realize how large this community was.

But I didn't speak to anyone. I tucked my yellow forms inside my bag, out of sight, just in case. I couldn't be a member of this community outdoors. As an MP and deputy party leader in an election year, the last thing I needed was for my fertility treatment to become public.

Besides, it didn't seem to be working.

Fertility treatment is a spectrum, which ranges from what you could call partial interventions to full-blown IVF. Some people, like us, work their way along the spectrum. One option fails, so try the next. Then the next. At first, with each failure, I could reassure myself. There is always the next option, and there will be one after that. It helped Clarke remain a constant optimist.

"It'll happen," he would tell me. "Don't worry." Never before had I experienced two words that felt quite as counterproductive as "don't worry." All the magazines and commentary warned against worrying: The more stress you have, the less likely you are to become pregnant.

But that just made me worry more. What if all this doesn't work? What if it doesn't, and if all treatments fail?

On July 26, I celebrated my thirty-seventh birthday by speaking at a business association in Tawa. They'd surprised me with a cake, iced in red and white, a cheerful nod to Labour colors. But they took great delight telling me, just as I sliced into it, that the cake itself was a bright blue, the color of the conservative movement. If you ask me, they laughed a little longer than was polite.

That was the state of things. We were two months from the 2017 election. Even with our new discipline, and our new team, even with John Key out of office and a new prime minister named Bill English, Labour remained the butt of jokes. We were polling in the mid-twenties, while the Green Party's vote increased. We had announced a plan to work together with the Greens, an attempt to strengthen the left bloc and put us in contention to form a government, but it wasn't enough yet.

I returned the Technicolor cake to the office and shared it. If I was going to be the target of someone's joke, the least I could do was hide it in the staff kitchen for others to enjoy.

Later that day, Andrew Little and I visited a film production company in Miramar. As we drove around Wellington's waterfront, we noticed Labour's campaign billboards, which were erected in public parks and intersections. The billboard showed me and Andrew standing side by side against a crimson background, with large white letters screaming A FRESH APPROACH. The motto had not been my pick. It reminded me of something you could see hanging inside a grocery store, as if Andrew and I were units of produce that consumers had to be persuaded to buy.

Not long later, Andrew and I were sitting in a darkened room talking screen industry strategy with several producers when our phones both chimed. We exchanged glances. Labour received weekly poll results, always in the late morning. The polls hadn't been good in a long time. However, the last few of polls have been fairly negative. I was scared that if nothing changed soon, we'd be in free fall.

I resumed the chat. But I couldn't help myself and pulled out my phone from beneath the table. When someone at the far end of the table started talking and no one was looking at me, I looked down.

Oh no.

I tried to maintain a poker face, but my heart felt like it had dropped into my stomach, and I couldn't concentrate on what was being said. Not after seeing the numbers. They were worse than I expected. Three-point drop in one week. We were polling at 23%, while the National Party had 42%. We weren't just looking at electoral defeat; we were looking at annihilation—the possibility of losing so many MPs that Labour, with its century-long history, would cease to be a legitimate major party. I kept hoping that the campaign's launch in just a few weeks would provide us with the platform we needed. And suddenly it appeared much more crucial.

The drive back to Parliament was quiet. When we arrived, Andrew dashed off to his office without saying goodbye. I sent him a quick text message: No matter how the polls turn out, I will always be optimistic about our chances. Everything will get better!

But when he responded, it was merely to let me know he wanted to talk.

Andrew's office was always frigid, and walking in made me shudder. Andrew stood behind his enormous oak desk, seemingly buried in contemplation. I moved to the couch and sat down, eager to hear what he required from me.

Andrew emerged from behind his desk and sat on the couch opposite me. I tried to sit more straight, but the couch drew me back into the cushions. Andrew still hadn't said anything. I looked up at the clock. It was around 2 p.m. The bells would ring at any moment, signaling that we needed to go to the debating room for question time.

Andrew cleared his throat. "I think I should stand down," he remarked. "And I think you should take over as leader."

I could hear discussions in the corridor, as MPs prepared to proceed to the house. Doors open and close. The whir of a printer. Andrew wants to step down. He believes I should take over. I went over his statements in my thoughts, trying to make them make sense.

I was not naive. I knew many saw me as a potential leader. Just weeks ago, a magazine ran a cover article with the heading Jacinda Ardern: Why She Is Our Prime Minister in Waiting. I'd even started popping up in favorite prime minister surveys, although with a meager 8 percent. But I'd also been in politics long enough to realize that commentators frequently promoted MPs as potential leaders. It was one thing to hear others conjecture. However, this was less than two months before the election. The advertisements had been filmed, and the billboards were up. It was too late for everything.

I sat in startled silence as Andrew stated that it might be in the best interests of the party. He did not believe he could win. He reasoned that if he stayed, we would lose too many MPs.

Even as he talked, a part of my mind was already racing ahead several weeks into the future. That portion of me was no longer seated in Andrew's office. Instead, I was standing in a darkened television studio, aware that millions of wide-eyed viewers were on the opposite side of the screen. Cameras in one studio faced two lecterns on a polished linoleum floor. Behind one lectern, the prime minister, Bill English, appeared serene and confident—not as personable as John Key, but pragmatic and calm, every bit the leader. I was behind the other lectern.

I pondered about the debates. The televised debates. I can't do them. I can't do any of it.

That was another reason why the public's speculation about my becoming leader was incorrect. None of the people who wrote those headlines or answered those poll questions knew what I did. If my first reaction when asked to take the baton was to list all the reasons why I couldn't, then I wasn't strong enough to lead.

I'm not sure what Andrew was saying when I eventually interrupted him. But I recall speaking eloquently and concisely. With a forceful voice, I explained why making changes right now was a bad idea. We needed steadiness. The celebration required it. The voters needed it.

When the campaign began, we were able to increase our numbers again. We only needed time. Time and consistency. I was in the middle of a sentence when the bells started chiming. We had five minutes to reach the debating hall. I stood up and prepared to go downstairs.
"We'll talk again?" I asked.
Andrew responded with a simple nod. I couldn't tell if I had convinced him to stay or if I had just convinced myself.
Six days later, I strolled into the Legislative Council Chamber, where twenty members of the media had come to wait. Microphones were on and cameras were rolling. I took my position in front of the microphones. Next to me stood Kelvin Davis, a former school principal, Te Tai Tokerau MP, and our newly elected deputy leader. Kelvin was a quiet person with rural roots whom Grant nominated for deputy and the caucus unanimously supported. Grant stood behind me, and other key Labour figures flanked my sides. I wore a black dress, a bright red blazer, and bright red lipstick. The hues of labor.
"Thank you everyone for joining us this afternoon," I blurted out. "I want to start by giving a brief statement." Flashbulbs went off, and I could hear camera shutters clicking. Don't doubt yourself; Annette had texted just a few months ago. Chin out and tell them you're ready.
"Following Andrew's statement this morning," I said, "I was nominated to lead the Labour Party. "My nomination was unanimously accepted."
I had been deputy leader for exactly five months. Now I was running for prime minister of New Zealand. There were times when I felt as if I was hovering above myself, seeing these fast-paced happenings. It everything felt quite weird. Or possibly, as one of my astonished colleagues exclaimed from the back of the caucus room after Andrew announced his resignation and instantly nominated me, "This is fucked!"
Andrew had brought me into his office six days ago and questioned his ability to continue as leader. Soon later, another poll was taken, this time in public. The pressure rose. In the days that followed, I still had no idea what Andrew was thinking, but in the back of my mind, I

began to play out the what-if scenarios. If he left, what would I say? If I were nominated, what would I do? What would the campaign look like if I was the leader?

And here I was. Andrew had resigned. I was now Labour's leader. And the election was only fifty-three days away.

I resumed my speech, utilizing a tactic I'd discovered years ago: if I talked loudly and strongly, I could keep my voice from shaking. I used the phrases "resolve," "steadfast," and "determined." I shared Labour's vision for New Zealand: that our country be a place where everyone has a roof over their heads and meaningful job, where education is free, where children grow up surrounded by creativity rather than hardship, and where we lead the world in environmental challenges. In other words, I intended to put kaitiakitanga into practice, to create a New Zealand that was better than we found it. I stated that Kelvin and I would be optimistic, organized, and prepared for the election—as if there weren't hundreds of billboards around the country showcasing the face of someone who was no longer party leader.

Then I took questions. They arrived immediately.

Do you think you are qualified for the position of Prime Minister?

What do you think will prepare you?

Do you feel you can establish a credible government with only 24 percent support?

Who are Jacinda Ardern and Kelvin Davis?

As I responded, I raised my head. I tried to exude a confidence that defied the questions I was asking. And then it ended. It was a quick and mostly happy start—25 minutes total—and the best I could have given us.

But none of this was going to be easy.

CHAPTER 13

I could relate to my swearing. I could tell you about the red-and-blue knee-length dress I wore, which was made of brocade. Or think about the bus, which I took with freshly minted ministers, people who seemed like family, from Government House to Parliament after a little ceremony with the governor general. I might explain that as we stepped off the bus, we heard saxophones, a trombone, and a constant rhythmic beat; a few members of Fat Freddy's Drop, a renowned Wellington band, were playing exuberantly at the base of the Parliament House stairs, and I thought, "This is the most Kiwi scene ever."

I could inform you about the crowds that day: Lining the forecourt, straining against the perimeter fencing, against the statue of former Premier Dick Seddon, and against one another. People dressed in suits and T-shirts, scarves and sunglasses, head covers and baseball caps, a riot of color under a clear blue sky.

I could tell you about the ceremonial events: speeches, warrant signings, and posing for official photos as if we were back in school. What it was like to glance behind me from the table at the swearing-in ceremony and see my father in his suit, exchanging texts with my mother, who was in London, where Louise had just given birth to a newborn boy named Alejandro. Then I walked into Parliament with Clarke and his nieces, the ones who had sat in high chairs when I first met his family—the bigger girl in Converse sneakers, the younger with her braids askew.

There was so much I could tell you about that day, but it all seemed like a blur, a gorgeous whirl of smiles, handshakes, and hugs, with cool air blowing through the bus windows.

So I'll tell you about a chat I had right before it all started. I was in the automobile on my way to Government House, where I would officially assume office. I was on the phone with John Campbell, a journalist I had been following since I was eleven. John wanted to catch me in the last few tranquil moments before everything changed.

He inquired how I was doing, and I responded as if it were any other day: "I'm OK, thank you. "How are you?"

"Well, I'm good," he replied, amused. "But I mean, I'm not driving to Government House to become the prime minister." Then he inquired where I was, and I told him I was near a Subway sandwich place. As we rounded the corner from Aitken to Mulgrave Street and passed by our national archives, a set of jackhammers started up.

"And when you return," he concluded, "you will be New Zealand's fortieth prime minister." Isn't that an exceptional thing?"

Well, yes. I assume it was.

John requested "one last idealistic flourish" from me before beginning the difficult task of governing. "Untethered, big-picture material. "What do you want to do?"

I'd answered questions like these a hundred times during the campaign. What is the plan? What is your agenda? I could recite a full work schedule off the cuff. However, that was not the first thing that came to mind.

"I want this government to feel different," I told them. "I want people to feel that it's open, that it's listening, and that it's going to bring kindness back."

"Kindness." That was the word. In some ways, it sounds like a child's word. Simple. Nonetheless, it contained everything that had left an impression on me: My father in his uniform in Murupara, agreed not to arrest a man just yet, especially in a town square, so that the individual can maintain some dignity. Hamish's wife cared for my mother as she came apart, and my mother cared for everyone. All the individuals I'd known throughout the years: family and friends, people I'd worshipped beside, worked with, and sometimes fought with, but always—always—for the greater good.

Some people felt kindness was mushy and squishy. A little naive, even. I knew it. But I also knew they were mistaken. Kindness has power and strength that nearly nothing else in the globe possesses. I had witnessed kindness accomplish remarkable things, such as give people hope, change minds, and transform lives. I wasn't afraid to speak it out loud, and I knew right away: kindness. This would be my guiding concept regardless of what lied ahead.

"Where are you now?" When John Campbell asked, I told him I was next to a KFC. We laughed and discussed a little more about what might change in the coming days, and how much. And by then, I was almost to Government House, and everything was about to start.

CHAPTER 14

Within a week, morning sickness crept in firmly and consistently—just like it did for my mother when she was pregnant with me and had to nurse Louise from the other side of the room. I was sick when my father and Clarke transported my few belongings from the studio apartment I'd been renting in Wellington to Premier House, the prime minister's mansion on the outskirts of Wellington's verdant greenbelt. I was nauseated when the manager of Premier House walked me through it for the first time—past conference rooms on the first level, into the prime minister's residential quarters on the second, all the decor eclectic and homey, patched together with furniture from all eras of New Zealand history. I wasn't nauseous to the point of rushing to the bathroom yet. I was able to nod excitedly as I was shown around the house—that's Muldoon's desk right there, there's the linen cabinet, and you'll find the civil defense kit in there—but my stomach was nauseous, my brain spinning, and my skin clammy.

It was worse when I awoke. Some mornings, as I got out of bed, the movement made my head spin. I'd race to the toilet and slump next to the bowl, hoping that the nausea would subside enough to allow me to get up off the floor. I could function and, more crucially, concentrate, but the vomiting was constant throughout the day.

It was there when our cabinet met for the first time, just hours after my swearing-in, and it was there in the days that followed as we hired staff and reviewed the many components of our hundred-day plan: an ambitious plan with nearly twenty different points of action, some of which required drafting or implementing new laws, while others, such as our plan to make the first year of university or polytechnic free, required entirely new systems.

Clarke stood in the door frame. "You okay?" In response to this query, I threw up again.

I wasn't fine. But I needed to be. Parliament opened today, marking the official resumption of administration under new leadership. My new leadership. It would be a magnificent spectacle, complete with pomp and ceremony. I moaned and felt the cool tile floor beneath me. I needed to get up.

I ran all upcoming events. First, all MPs would march in a formal parade to the debating chamber. Then our new speaker, Trevor Mallard, would enter, accompanied by the sergeant at arms, carrying the ceremonial mace that reflects Parliament's authority. Meanwhile, on the forecourt, a public location in front of Parliament used for both celebrations and protests, the Defence Force would gather, with Royal Air Force trumpeters sounding their horns as the governor-general arrived. Following the national anthem and soldier inspection, the governor-general and her party will enter Parliament House with a traditional pōwhiri and haka. The entire ceremony would be steeped in history and formality, from the diplomatic corps to judges and ministers. Unless of course it rained. In this instance, everyone would simply stroll inside.

The entire day would end with the giving of one speech, formally known as the "speech from the throne." The governor-general read this address, which was drafted by the government, including myself and my team. The speech from the throne officially informed Parliament of the agenda it would consider for the next three years. It foreshadowed what legislation we would enact, which domestic issues we would prioritize, and even how we would approach the international scene. We were a coalition government (Labour, Greens, and New Zealand First), so writing this speech wasn't simple.

We had spent weeks working on it. We'd even brought in Heather Simpson, H2, to assist us. Heather was well-versed in both the Greens and New Zealand First, and she was instrumental in guiding us through the speech's text. I'd once been intimidated by her intelligence and demeanor, so it felt strange to see her standing behind the prime minister's desk, exactly as she had when I was a twenty-four-year-old junior adviser. This time, however, I was sitting at the desk, with a pile of salt and vinegar chips nearby.

With all these events just hours away, I flushed the toilet and got up from the floor. What if I vomit today during the state opening? What the hell am I gonna do?

Clarke brought me water and extra crackers. I moved gently. I put on tights, a navy-blue dress with an abstract pattern, and a black blazer over top. I willed my stomach to relax. I arrived at the event, took steady steps, and held my head up high. Before long, the chamber was full of all 120 MPs. At the front of the chamber were people dressed in military uniforms, traditional attire, judicial robes and wigs, and the governor-general, who sat in a regal-looking high-backed seat and faced the audience. The governor-general motioned for people to sit, which prompted me to step up from my seat beside her and offer her the speech she would read. As soon as I took my place, she said, "It is a privilege for me to exercise Her Majesty the Queen's prerogative and open the 52nd Parliament." I'm not sure; it could have been the act of standing. But that was when I realized I needed to vomit.

The back of my throat felt constricted, nearly choking. My lips watered, indicating that my stomach could not contain even the smallest amount of food. I planned my escape route: a door on the right and a washroom in the ayes lobby. But I was aware that I would be televised live, and a prime minister cannot simply leave the throne in the middle of a speech. Do not throw up. Do not throw up. Do not throw up.

I was able to pull it together enough to make it through the ceremony, but this would recur again in the coming weeks. I was meeting foreign dignitaries at the Beehive while also chairing caucus sessions and holding news conferences. I was sick so frequently that I came to equate the fragrance of the ninth floor with sickness. Before long, every time I got off of the lift, a wave slammed me.

Finally, I called my general practitioner. Julia and Clarke were the only people who knew I was pregnant, so my doctor opened her office after hours and gave me nausea meds. Even when I questioned her about whether they could harm the baby, I realized I had no choice but to take them.

Then came the next challenge. "You'll need a scan," she added. She had an old friend and colleague, an obstetrician in nearby Mount Eden, whom she trusted to be discreet. She took up the phone. "I can send him a text, connect you both, and you can take it from there."

We were driving along Mount Eden Road on a Sunday night, with the unmarked police car that had been following us everywhere these days trailing behind. At least we were alone in our automobile. The fast journey provided an opportunity to devise a strategy for when we arrived at the obstetrician's office. Even the guards had no idea what we were doing here. The more people who knew, the more likely it was to leak to the press, and I'd find myself discussing having a baby only a few weeks into the job. "So, what's our story again?" Clarke asked me.

"I told the protection officers that we were just off for a quick catch-up with a friend." I'd spoken with the obstetrician, Nick Walker, earlier that day. He had a complete plan. We should park in front of his offices, where it is "dark, quiet, with lots of parking," and stroll to the back of the building. He'd meet us at the back entrance. He was sure no one would see us at that late hour, especially on a weekend. Nobody, that is, save the diplomatic protection service (DPS), a group of professionally trained police officers who kept track of my every move in a little notebook. And, as far as they knew, it was simply a visit with an old buddy who happened to be working over the weekend.

A few days later, I awoke frozen. For a second, I had no idea where I was. Light filtered through the thin slats over the window.

Vietnam. I'm in Vietnam. I lay back down for a bit, cautious not to get up too quickly, and went over the plan I'd devised the night before. Get up. Shower. Cover myself with tropical strength. DEET insect repellent applies from head to toe. Reread my briefings.

This was my first abroad journey, to attend the Asia-Pacific Economic Cooperation (APEC) leaders' conference. New Zealand's international reputation is a source of great pride for the country. When people talk about us on the global stage, they use expressions like "punching above our weight" in an attempt to convey that, despite our small size, we have never shied away from being honest about matters. Two days after Hitler invaded Poland, we were one of the first four countries to declare war on Germany. Since then, we've resisted nuclear testing, apartheid, and the Iraq War. We were the world's first country to grant women the right to vote. We had spoken out in support of human rights, labor legislation, and the advantages of fair trade. As leader, I served as an ambassador for my country, responsible for our reputation and legacy. That obligation felt really essential.

This year's APEC gathering in Vietnam was very important. It coincided with the final stages of negotiating the Comprehensive and Progressive pact for Trans-Pacific Partnership (CPTPP), a poorly termed but important trade pact for New Zealand. During the election, Labour advocated for more protections for us in the agreement. I now needed to deliver. All while avoiding mosquitos.

By the time I was scheduled to leave for Vietnam and subsequently the Philippines, Zika cases were still being reported. Zika was transmitted by mosquito bites. Zika is not very hazardous for non-pregnant individuals. However, for those who are, it can cause severe birth problems such as microcephaly, which occurs when the front of a baby's skull is malformed and brain development is impeded. I was in my first trimester of a secret pregnancy and very scared about Zika. At the conference, I ran from one meeting room to the next, mercifully with air conditioning to keep both the insects and my sickness at bay. On my first day, I had three breakfast meetings and ate nearly nothing. I'm not a vegetarian, but I told folks I was when abroad. It seemed less noticeable than mentioning all the things a pregnant lady should avoid. I quickly learned to walk quickly, stick with the locally assigned protection team, and always wear my pin—which informed security that I was a leader and was supposed to be inside an otherwise tightly controlled perimeter and meetings attended by Presidents Xi Jinping, Vladimir Putin, and Donald Trump.

Becoming Prime Minister is a weird experience. Sometimes the strange experiences are minor and insignificant—like my first night in

Premier House, when I ordered takeaway from an Indian restaurant down the street but they didn't produce the order, figuring that "Jacinda Ardern, Premier House" was an obvious fraud. Or the same night, when I went looking for linens and discovered helmets and flak jackets among extra duvet covers and towels. Or when I attempted to take an Uber to an Aldous Harding concert, only to be told by security that I was "not to use that mode of transport anymore please, ma'am."

Other times, however, momentous moments strike you more forcefully, such as when I entered a room full of other foreign leaders and thought, There's Donald Trump, not on a screen, but right in front of me, looking taller than I imagined, his tan more prominent. Vladimir Putin is silent, generally alone, and nearly expressionless. And Justin Trudeau extended his arm to meet me with a handshake before introducing me to Michelle Bachelet, Chile's president and one of the few women in the room who has lived through a dictatorship. They are all wearing the same gold pins that announce to the world that they, like me, are in power of a country. The strange feeling of the encounter lasted only an instant before disappearing. There was work to do.

Now, Prime Minister Abe was leading a last-ditch effort to move the CPTPP forward. By then, negotiations were tense. David Parker, our new trade minister, was there with me, and while we had made progress, we were still unsure whether the agreement would be completed.

I passed through groups of officials and security on my way to the meeting with Malcolm Turnbull, Australia's prime minister, who was authoritative, no-nonsense, and, like me, bent on finalizing the trade agreement. As we strolled, we discussed the most recent developments in negotiations, with officials dashing past in either direction on a crowded path. When we arrived in the conference room, Malcolm strolled straight through. But before I could enter, security guards on either side lowered their arms in front of me, preventing me from entering.

"I'm sorry, I'm supposed to be in there," I said, aware that they'd clearly concluded that I wasn't a leader but still wanted to be polite about it. But the crowd in the hallway was too dense and loud for them to hear me. Furthermore, they had ceased looking at me at this point; they were too preoccupied with keeping an eye out for the next impostor, while their arms continued to serve as a barrier.

I was debating my next move when I felt a hand wrap around my arm. Malcolm had reached back past the security officers and was now tugging me from the opposite side.

"She is the prime minister of New Zealand!" he exclaimed, outraged on my behalf. It was only then that I looked down and realized what had happened. My long hair obscured my pin, and aside from that shiny marking, there was nothing that made me appear particularly leader-like. And perhaps less so at a gathering where I was one of just three female leaders, together with Hong Kong's Carrie Lam and Michelle Bachelet.

Moments like this have never surprised me. Not even at home. A few months after my swearing-in, I went down to the Parliament cafeteria to eat dinner. When I requested the employee behind the desk to put it on my account, she stared at me and asked for my name. I had told her about Jacinda Ardern. She looked at her list of accounts. "Can you spell that, please?" I accomplished it, although my protection officer was struggling to hold back his laughs. Keeping it genuine, I thought, laughing along.

Near the end of my Vietnam trip, I hopped into the back seat of the car with GJ, my acting chief of staff. I smelled of DEET. When the doors closed and the car started rolling, I noticed a mosquito trapped in the back. The reasonable portion of my brain understood that the chances of this mosquito carrying Zika were slim. Only sixty-eight pregnant women had been afflicted in Vietnam thus far. But in the last six months, I had become Labour Party leader, been sworn in as Prime Minister, and become pregnant despite doctors' warnings that I would not. I no longer believed in the concept of modest odds.

It was mid-January. My first hundred days had not yet expired, but we had already made the first year of university or apprenticeship free, established an interim climate commission, and passed legislation to extend paid maternity leave. I was twenty weeks pregnant. Summer had given me the advantage of open blouses, but concealing my expanding midsection was becoming difficult.

Now it's time to spread the word. I was terrified that the country would respond like my grandfather had.

How was this going to land? For three months, I had been replaying that question in my thoughts, obtaining different responses each time. Throughout my career, I thought I had a good sense of how people would react to various situations. On this matter, however, I had lost all perspective. Some days, I convinced myself that others would be happy for me. Others I was confident that whatever chance I had of being a good leader would be dashed by the commentary "PM prioritizes family over country."

During our final week of summer vacation, a good buddy who worked in politics and communication came to visit. He and I talked about a mutual friend who had lately informed us of her own pregnancy. "I had always hoped we'd have babies at the same time," I explained. Then, after a moment, I casually asked, "What do you think people would say if that happened?"

My pal had chuckled. "I don't think it would go down well."

"Yeah," I answered, laughing as if the question had been a completely hypothetical thinking experiment. "Yeah…"

But at this point, it didn't matter what others said. I informed a few colleagues and then devised a strategy for spreading the word further. First, I'd meet Winston. I'd tell him that he'd need to take over as prime minister for the six weeks I planned to be on maternity leave. Others needed to be told, too: The Governor-General. The Green party. My caucus colleagues. And friends, whom I believed should hear it from me rather than the media.

Finally, I would inform the country.

When the big day arrived, we executed the plan with military precision, including a press statement and a synchronized Instagram announcement. We chose a basic graphic. Two fishing hooks placed side by side. In the center of the second one was a little hook—a baby hook. The caption stated, "And we thought 2017 was a great year! Clarke and I are very happy that in June... I will be Prime Minister and a mother, while Clarke will be the 'first man of fishing' and a stay-at-home father. I know there will be a lot of questions, and we will address them all. But for today, welcome 2018."
I clicked post and then waited.

CHAPTER 15

Clarke and I organized a press conference 72 hours following the birth of our daughter, Neve, to introduce her to the world. We prepared everything before I gave birth, and I was confident it would be alright. I thought Kate Middleton did it. I can make it work.

It didn't feel good now since I had just given birth.

I'd spent the most of my waking hours since Neve arrived staring at her, as new parents do. I had waited and fretted for so long, and now she was finally here. I felt relieved and elated.

My physique, however, was another story. Even the easiest birth may split a body in two, and Neve's wasn't. Her pulse rate had plummeted dramatically near the end of labor, and she had emerged with the chord wrapped around her neck. Her first night, she'd been awake for twelve hours straight, which meant I had, too. I was almost delirious from a lack of sleep.

I had also rarely changed out of my jammies since she was born. My hair was unwashed, and the best option was to draw it back into a bun. My postpartum stomach was, should we say, not small. Walking any distance made me feel as if my insides were falling out.

Perhaps the most unsettling aspect of it all was the posters on the maternity unit's walls warning me that I might be suddenly overwhelmed with overwhelming emotions. I didn't feel like that was going to happen. I was just so exhausted. But the visuals made me feel as if I could burst into tears without warning, enormous powerful cries, like a spontaneous garden sprinkler.

I had Neve in my arms. She was wrapped in a blanket knit by Clarke's mother and wore a small green knit cap given to us by my seasoned midwife, Libby. Clarke appeared next me, beaming in a woolen cardigan with a southwestern pattern. He didn't look like the man who had uncomfortably hugged his new infant nephew a few years ago. Then he seemed more comfortable clutching a crawfish.

Now he looked like a father.

I didn't tell the media everything, of course. I didn't tell them that the hospital room I'd been living in had a small vestibule at the door for protection officers, since it was intended to house detained inmates from the neighboring Mount Eden prison who would require hospital treatment. I didn't tell them that Clarke had snuck past the media while I was in labor to buy me a lemonade Popsicle, or that the first meal I had after the birth—Marmite on toast with a cup of Milo—was possibly the best meal of my life. I didn't tell them what Clarke had told me: that the first time I held Neve, I looked like a crazy person, wide-eyed with joy, and that I then asked him how he would have looked after that labor. Instead, as I faced the cameras and microphones in front of me, I simply stated that it was a pleasure to welcome our child to the country.

After that, I wanted to go inside and tuck Neve into her car seat before leaving the hospital for home. But there were other questions. I rocked back and forth on my feet, striving to keep everything where it belonged—organs, emotions, bodily fluids—while answering a second question. This one came from a television journalist.

Then there was the difficulty with sleep. Neve slept well during the day while I tried to work—because even with Winston temporarily in charge, and even though I had things as structured as possible, there were still paperwork to examine, political matters to be involved in, and plans to weigh in on. So I joined conference meetings with Neve on my lap, attempting to balance two separate worlds.

By night, Neve was restless—a "party baby," as Clarke called her. At first, the days became fuzzy. However, after a few weeks, the insomnia took a new form. Being woken up so frequently made me physically uncomfortable that I began to dread the night.

And then, at some point, my sleep-deprived brain determined that the best option was to avoid trying to sleep at all. Simply stay awake. So I watched Netflix between feedings. Alone in the dark, I attempted to watch a few tough crime shows, which I like before Neve arrived, but they all made me irrationally upset. So I switched to Unbreakable Kimmy Schmidt instead. Before I fell asleep, I had a dream that I was within the show, in Kimmy's basement apartment, with Titus Andromedon styling me.

There was also the plain reality of physical healing. I expected more twists and turns after finding out I was pregnant and being labeled as a geriatric mom. But it also made me marvel a little more. My thirty-seven-year-old body had created this entire human being and supported the two of us for nine months. It eventually got her airside, wide-eyed and perfectly developed. However, this did not mean that my body was content to just recover as needed. For weeks afterward, I struggled to stand fully upright. I'd stroll around my house in a circuit, somewhat stooped from the sense that nothing had been put back together. I wondered if this was how I would be from now on.

But as the weeks passed, Neve's evenings became a little easier, and her intervals between awakenings grew longer. The formula helped, and my fixation with feeding subsided somewhat. I began to walk a little further and more upright. By the time I was able to do those things, six weeks had passed.

Amidst all this history, Neve and I created our own mark. The house management renovated an end-of-hall room into a nursery. When we arrived, a blanket with a giraffe sewn across the front lay inside an old wooden cot, and on the spare bed beside were knit gifts and embroidered pillows bearing Neve's name, many of which had been given by well-wishers from all over the country. This old residence has housed numerous prime ministers. For the first time, it was home to a child born to a single parent.

We had a new regimen. Most weeks, Clarke, Neve, and I flew between Premier House and our home in Auckland. Clarke looked after Neve during the day, walking her to the Beehive—a ten-minute walk in excellent weather—several times a day so I could nurse at my desk or in the kitchen adjacent to my office. When Clarke had to go for filming, Mum, or Clarke's mother, would come and stay.

I've heard numerous times that having your own children makes you appreciate your mother even more. But I didn't simply appreciate my mother; I relied on her. She was always there for us, and she made being a working mom enjoyable. She jotted down the funniest things Neve did and said. She frequently sent cheerful texts from Neve in the first person, as if Neve herself was drafting the message: "Morning mum, I had a good nap this morning like a good girl!" Mum continued to dress Neve in the frilliest hand-me-downs she could locate. Mum arrived in Wellington one day with a pink-and-white frock with an exaggerated collar and piping at the hem—one of my old baby costumes that she had supposedly been storing all these years, ready to dress my child as she had previously clothed me.

We had a village, and we were making things work.

Then, a month after my maternity leave ended, I went on my first international trip without Neve, to the Pacific Islands Forum in Nauru. Bringing her was not a possibility since she was too young and the journey was too long—an overnight flight with one day on the ground. I traveled to Nauru with my pumps, sterilizing tablets, and a refrigerated bin. Nauru is the world's third-smallest country by landmass, surrounded by gorgeous blue seas that, like most Pacific islands, make it highly sensitive to the effects of climate change. Extreme weather events have become an existential threat that people were monitoring in real time.

This was unquestionably an essential meeting that I needed to attend, but it was also my first time away from Neve. So I did what I typically do when faced with the conflicting demands of two responsibilities: I didn't think about it. I set up compartments. I had a job to complete. One that, for the most part, required being in a meeting room, but occasionally required being linked to a pump in a side room with a slew of equipment and a chilly bin nearby. Both jobs were important, needed to be completed, and came with a lot of baggage.

Then, in September, just weeks after the Pacific Islands Forum, I was scheduled to appear before the United Nations General Assembly. I knew exactly what I wanted to talk about: the climate issue, its impact on our region, and the dire need for governments to collaborate on solutions, as leaders in Nauru and atolls such as Tokelau had requested.

Because a trip to New York City is too long for a breastfeeding mother to do alone, Clarke, Neve, and I boarded a thirteen-hour Air New Zealand flight that flew through the night from Auckland to Houston, then another three and a half hours to JFK. By the time we arrived at our hotel, it was one a.m. in New York and dinnertime in New Zealand.

A few days later, I spoke at a Nelson Mandela memorial gathering in the General Assembly. Clarke and Neve gathered in the wings in case Neve needed to be fed. By now, she had gratefully adjusted to the time zone difference.

When I finished speaking, we all sat together in New Zealand's allotted seating area on the General Assembly floor, my gaze shifting between Neve and the other speakers. That's when I heard "click, click, click." I moved awkwardly. I couldn't see where the noise was coming from until our high commissioner pointed up at a row of booths above the floor. "There's a few media up there," he remarked.

Still not realizing it was us they were interested in, I made goofy expressions at Neve while Clarke held her. By the end of the day, these photographs would have spread worldwide.

These photos document the first occasion a newborn was taken to the floor of the United Nations General Assembly. But when I look at them—Neve's double chin, cheeks bursting around the pacifier in her mouth, her blue-and-white-striped outfit, a hand-me-down from Louise that Neve would outgrow in weeks—I don't think of the historic occasion.

Instead, I consider the persons right outside the camera frame: The foreign policy adviser who babysat so we could attend an event with the US president. The high commissioner who discovered bassinets, sterilizers, and Jolly Jumpers to transform his residence into a playpen. Clarke changed Neve's nappies, soothed her to sleep, and accompanied me around for feeding.

Women should not have to choose between being good at their jobs and being decent moms or daughters, as our mothers frequently did. There should be support networks, a village, or whatever you want to call it, that can help them be all of those things while not losing themselves entirely. That's what I was fortunate to have at the UN and elsewhere: the affection and support of others. And today, that's exactly what I reply when someone brings up that photo at the UN or stops me in the store to ask how I did it.

The UN trip was momentous, but it was also heartbreaking. On the second day, I observed that Neve was fussing whenever I tried to feed. Clarke, Neve, and I were in a changing room adjacent to the auditorium before my address at Columbia University. The area was vacant, with white cinderblock walls and bench seats. People offered to help us all the time—did I need tea, a restroom, a more comfortable spot to sit, my bag, my speech notes, help with my outfit, or help with my baby? No thank you, I replied. I was just about to feed my baby before go onstage.

I was not giving up breastfeeding, but Neve was. She'd had enough of feeding when I was present. From my inconsistent supply. About my sometimes hasty attitude to everything. But I didn't want to concede because I thought it meant I was failing. It also meant that I would no longer have an excuse to have Neve with me, whether on the road or at work.

There were fresh things to be concerned about: lower-than-expected GDP figures, a minister being investigated for his handling of an immigration matter, and a complaint and report regarding one of our police officers. There wasn't enough time, not enough hours in the day, which is a common problem for all mothers.

I peered in at Neve. She was totally asleep in her sleeping bag. I shut the door to her room, walked into mine, climbed into bed, and drew the blankets up around me. Twenty-eighteen had been a long year.

"Next year," I explained to Clarke. "Next year will be easier."

CHAPTER 16

On Friday, March 15, 2019, I awoke thinking about hydrogen.

I was on my way to New Plymouth, Harry's former neighborhood, to launch what we had been dubbing a "hydrogen road map." A few months after becoming Prime Minister, I announced that New Zealand would no longer issue new permits for offshore oil and gas development. My reasoning was straightforward: if we needed to move away from fossil fuels, we needed to cease looking for them.

Environmentalists and climate activists cheered the announcement, but in New Plymouth, New Zealand's oil and gas powerhouse, reactions ranged from skepticism to open hatred. Neil Holdom, New Plymouth's mayor—a nice guy with a protective, well-intentioned spirit that reminded me of a high school principal—once told me I made him want to hide under his desk.

However, in my perspective, a change did not imply the end of an industry and all that it included. I remembered what happened in Murupara in the 1980s, when the forestry business changed dramatically. We realized New Plymouth required an alternative long-term plan, which is where hydrogen came in.

Andrew Little, the former Labour leader who gave I the reins shortly before the election's accompany me for the day. Andrew served as both our justice minister and the MP for New Plymouth. Our energy minister, Megan Woods, would also speak at the hydrogen summit, where the plan would be unveiled. Megan was one of our most determined ministers. If there was something difficult to do, she was one of the persons to delegate it to. On the ninth floor, we frequently joked that she would have been as at ease as a military major as an MP. Megan's hard work and unwavering determination had guided us through the oil and gas choice, and she had been a strong supporter of the hydrogen endeavor.

The rest of the day was planned. I'd go to a green school with Mayor Holdom. In the evening, I'd go to the World of Music, Arts, and Dance (WOMAD) festival's opening ceremony. Clarke would accompany me to WOMAD while my aunt Marie babysat Neve. It was going to be a hectic day, even before I added my own unexpected stop, which I hadn't informed anyone about.

Kelly climbed into the van next to me, where Andrew and Megan were already waiting. In front of us sat a member of my security team. "Now I know we haven't planned this," I murmured, taking my seat. "But we should stop by the student strike."

Kelly was unmoved, as I had predicted. "I knew you'd say that," she said, smiling as she picked up her phone. Meanwhile, my protection officer began chatting down his sleeve, as they did every time I disturbed a meticulously planned strategy. We soon found ourselves in front of the city center plaza.

I'd previously heard that hundreds of young people were coming into Wellington's Parliament courtyard. James Shaw, our climate minister and Green Party co-leader, was scheduled to speak. I was wondering if James would be able to make an appearance after being assaulted by a conspiracy theorist on his way to work the day before. The man attacked James outside the botanic gardens, striking him several times and yelling about the UN. We had spoken, and while I knew he was fine, I was still stunned by the brutality and randomness of it all, and I was concerned for James.

Raj, my acting chief of staff, had dealt with the matter. I had hired Raj from the corporate sector to return to politics and manage our team of advisers. When my chief of staff had to stand aside owing to illness, Raj stepped in. He was quiet, focused, and one of the most dedicated workers I know. But, beneath his cool demeanor, I realized he was in politics for the same reasons I was. He was now working through questions about MPs' safety and security. One of the reasons I hadn't discussed my change of plans with my crew on the ninth floor was that they already had plenty going on. Besides, I understood they'd rather I didn't enter a position where I might be booed. It was a risk I was ready to take, particularly because I agreed with the students.

The hydrogen summit was a straightforward affair, with speakers followed by a brief press conference. Megan had left for the airport at

1:40, while Kelly and Andrew Little had gotten back into the van. As we drove to the green school, Mayor Holdom and I sat next to the protection officer in the front seat.

I was feeling good, as I typically do after finishing the "hard stuff" for the day. The summit went well, the press conference was uneventful, and the school strike for climate left me feeling inspired.

We were rattling down rural roads, Mayor Holdom and I discussing the summit, Andrew sitting calmly as Kelly took phone calls in the backseat. The air was pleasant, and the gloomy sky that morning appeared to be clearing. Green pastures with grazing animals appeared and disappeared outside our window.

I pushed the phone to my ear, listening to my chief press secretary, Andrew Campbell, recount the information as he received it.

A shooting occurred. Three persons are confirmed dead. Parts of Christchurch, including schools, are under lockdown. It is unknown whether there are many assailants or sites.

By now, the van had lurched to the side of the road and performed a wide U-turn. I turned to face the mayor. He was completely silent, staring straight ahead. "I'm so sorry," I blurted foolishly, as if the significance of the van's abrupt about-face wasn't clear. "I'm afraid we won't be making that school visit."

I made further phone calls. The Minister of Police. The Deputy Prime Minister. Then Clarke. Andrew Campbell suggested that this may be coordinated. Clarke answered the first ring, his voice loud.

"Neve had a good nap," he announced joyfully. "We've just arrived at a café for a bit of lunch."

I told him they had to return to the hotel.

"What? Leave? Why? I've just ordered a beef pie."

I simply told him the basics: an attack, possibly several, a mosque, and a lot of unknowns. In my mind's eye, I could see him handling the pram and Neve's nappy bag, attempting to put together the terribly scant information I'd provided him. Most days, Clarke received half-stories from me, with the blanks left for him to fill in.

Frequently, I communicated nothing at all, only to later become irritated that he hadn't picked up on the gravity of whatever ambiguous circumstance I was in. I knew I was doing it again, but I also wanted him to hurry.

"Please, my love," I asked. "Please just go back to the hotel."

I was desperate for knowledge. What could people tell me about what was going on? After twenty minutes, the van arrived at the New Plymouth police headquarters parking area, which had a high wire fence and barbed wire around the top. There was enough time to determine that two mosques were involved, that there were unsubstantiated reports of a shooting at a hospital, and that the death toll was rapidly increasing. Everything seemed so precarious. Details were blurry, and nothing settled in my mind. Not in terms of magnitude or meaning. Not yet.

In the parking lot, I quickly bid goodbye to the mayor and Andrew Little.

"I hope you can find your way back." Before they could respond, protective services had already led Kelly and me into the station. I expected the station to be packed with bustle, but Kelly and I discovered a ghost floor. A massive area, full with workstations and cubicles, but strangely unoccupied. The light was dim, muffled by the window screens. The room was silent, no phone ringing. We walked via a public kitchen to the police sergeant's office on the far end of the floor, where I expected to be briefed. But his office was also deserted. That's when I understood I was not looking for information. I was here because the cops wanted to protect me. I felt immediately restless and agitated. I didn't know who to ask or who to dispute with about leaving the small room Kelly and I were in. I knew the cops were doing their thing, but I had to do mine. And as long as I was in a police station, isolated from the individuals who could brief me and the knowledge I needed to make decisions, I was rendered useless. I sat in the sergeant's office when my phone rang.

It was Andrew, again. "There's a manifesto," he explained. Through the phone, I could hear hurried talk and printer hums. "The shooter wrote a manifesto, and he sent it to us."

I was holding a pen and had paper on a coffee table in front of me, but I had stopped jotting down notes.

There were so many holes in my knowledge of the shooting. I still didn't know how many people had been injured or killed. But now I understood why someone had opened fire on a congregation of innocent people at their place of worship. All of my bewilderment and fury combined into a single emotion: blinding rage.

After hanging up with Andrew, I rose up, exited the sergeant's office, and went to the elevator well. I started pacing. This was practically impossible to understand. A manifesto. A prepared attack. So much hate. I was going to have to communicate information with the country and ensure that people felt peaceful and protected, although the attacker's objective was to make everyone afraid and fearful. I walked back and forth in front of the elevator. I needed to focus. To create a plan. And there was only one person I wanted to accomplish this with. When no one came to the police station, I asked the protection officers whether we might leave. My press conference would be at the hotel. Now, just before I was supposed to speak, I walked by our hotel room, where Neve was sleeping and Clarke was watching live reporting on television with the sound turned down. We locked eyes and stared at each other for a long time, stunned and silent. Then my gaze shifted to the television screen.

It showed an ambulance with lights flashing outside a Christchurch hospital. Ambulance doors were open and a man was being taken from the rear. I couldn't see his face, but the movement in his body indicated that he was alert and alive. As the stretcher was wheeled into the hospital door, the guy raised his arm, reaching skyward to his God, his Creator, as if making a desperate appeal.

Until now, the reports I'd heard were all verbal. These were realities, not images. Human beings are not numbers. It wasn't like seeing folks lying ill or hurt made it any more real than the moment Kelly handed me the phone in the van. But from that point forward, anything else I felt was replaced by a sorrow so profound that there are no words to explain it, even years later.

But I had five minutes to find any words. Five minutes before I addressed the nation.

On the television screen, the man vanished through the hospital doors. I watched another ambulance arrive. And another.

I took up the piece of paper on which I had rapidly jotted down bullet points. It was the opposite side of a page I had created for the hydrogen summit.

I'd disclose facts. Only that which had been confirmed. However, I realized that facts alone would not enough.

My pen flew across the page. This is an act of unparalleled, unprecedented violence. It has no place in New Zealand.

The press room had a high ceiling and black carpet, resembling a venue used for conferences and weddings where people ate buffet meals and danced all night. Today, however, it was empty. A black tablecloth covered a table on the far side of the room. Two microphones, six Dictaphones, and a water bottle were arranged in the center.

A press conference often consists of reporters from many television and radio stations, three or four print journalists, and an equal number of cameras. But I was in New Plymouth, hours from any major metropolis. Today, two camera operators and four journalists were sitting in front of me. They were silent.

Later that night, in my Wellington office, I picked up the phone and called Gamal Fouda, the imam at Al Noor mosque, where the majority of the deaths had happened.

On the other end of the line, I heard a tiny sound, the smallest conceivable hint that he was present and heard me. I imagined him standing amid the chaos and sadness, with desperate families all around him. I reflected on everything he had seen, everything he could never unsee.

"I am sorry," I said. "I am so sorry."

Again, he reacted with a little noise. So I repeated it once more. I said it till I was confident he had heard me.

"I am so, so sorry."

CHAPTER 17

The March 15 terrorist attack used six firearms, including two AR-15-style rifles, a semiautomatic, and a pump-action shotgun. The terrorist had legally obtained his weapons and then modified them to make them even more lethal.

He was not a citizen. He was a newcomer to New Zealand, having arrived only 18 months before. Nonetheless, we had granted him permission to employ weaponry intended solely for the objective of killing as many people as possible in the shortest amount of time.

There is no constitutional right to own firearms in New Zealand. But gun ownership is not uncommon. According to some estimates, our gun-ownership-to-population index is seventeenth in the globe, putting us firmly within the top ten percent of all nations. New Zealanders learn to use guns to hunt deer, goats, and other pests, much as I had to cope with possums on our orchard.

Over the years, attempts have been made to reform gun laws. The majority had either not traveled very far or had gone nowhere. Some of the most significant developments occurred in the early 1990s, shortly after the Aramoana incident, which, until March 15, had been the largest mass shooting in New Zealand history: a man involved in a neighbor's dispute killed thirteen people. However, while the post-Aramoana revisions required additional processes to obtain certain firearms, no weapons were prohibited.

But now the unspeakable had occurred. I was determined that our gun regulations would change. And we had a model that we could use.

In 1996, a mass shooting occurred at Port Arthur in Tasmania, Australia. The perpetrator utilized two semiautomatic rifles. While the motivation for the attack differed from that of Christchurch, the death toll was significant. 35 persons were shot and murdered. The conservative Australian prime leader at the time, John Howard, acted immediately to outlaw pump-action, semiautomatic, and automatic firearms. He also instituted a buyback scheme and an amnesty for anyone who possessed the outlawed firearms. I understood there was no reason to reinvent the wheel. We might adopt Australia's reform as an example.

Raj collaborated with a small team on an early briefing to outlaw military-style semiautomatic guns. Meanwhile, officials from the New Zealand Police and the Minister of Police's office worked tirelessly to produce the necessary paperwork. Within three days after the shooting, the cabinet agreed in principle to proceed with reforms.

However, reform is not a general concept. It needs a commitment to specificity, such as definitions, standards, and procedures. Sometimes this necessitated making judgment calls. Our focus was on high-capacity weaponry, but how would we define "high" capacity? Duck hunters frequently utilized pump-action shotguns. These are also among the most commonly used pest-control weapons on farms. Some pump-action shotguns have five-round magazines. Others, ten rounds. How many did a hunter or farmer need? We debated the difference between significant reform and an undue burden on this issue.

Five days after the March 15 assault, I met with emergency personnel in Christchurch. We sat in a locker room at the police station, where the specialized Armed Offenders Squad met and donned protective gear when a situation necessitated an armed response. My visit's objective was straightforward: to express gratitude. While it was two senior constables named Jim and Scott who bravely detained the armed shooter as he was on his way to a third mosque, the Armed Offenders Squad was heavily involved that day.

They sat on seats in front of their lockers as I spoke. They were quiet, with their heads down. I concluded my sentence and began to leave. Then an idea came to me. "I have a quick question," I said, turning back to face them. "How many of you hunt?" Almost all hands went up.

"And I'm guessing many of you use pump-action shotguns?"

Most people nodded. They did.

"Maybe you can help me," I said. "If you're a hunter or farmer, how many rounds should a pump-action shotgun have? If you were to rewrite the legislation, where would the cutoff be?

No one was better qualified to consider the subject than this collection of people. They wielded weapons and confronted weapons. They were both recreational hunters and professional first responders to incidents involving armed criminals.

Their stillness quickly gave way to a spirited conversation. They discussed the reasons for a five-round cutoff vs a ten-round cutoff, taking into account the ramifications for both public safety and a good duck hunt.

Finally, they agreed.

"Five rounds," one said, and the others nodded. "You do not need ten for a hunt. "Five will do."

I thanked them. The event may have been unplanned, but this was the most knowledgeable, intelligent focus group I could have gathered, and I was grateful. When I got in the car, I called the team. "I think we have an answer to our shotgun issue."

Seventeen days after the shooting, we submitted the new law to Parliament. Ten days later, the law prohibiting military-style semiautomatic firearms passed with the support of all but one member of parliament. The bill established an amnesty and buyback program, allowing anyone who had the weapons we had just declared illegal to be paid for turning them in.

Ten thousand firearms were surrendered to authorities within the first month of the law's passage. These transactions were simple. We created collection points. People brought their forbidden firearms. In exchange, cash was transferred into their accounts. Then they headed home.

By the end of the year, 56,000 firearms and approximately 200,000 gun parts will have been turned in and destroyed.

More sensible gun reforms would still be necessary, but we would not win every battle. A gun registration program we introduced later—allowing officials to know how many guns, and what type, gun owners owned, as well as medical professionals to know if a patient was at risk from weapons at home—would also pass, but with less unanimity, putting the policy at risk of being overturned by future Parliaments.

But we had acted. We had done something. Equally important, we had demonstrated that something could be done.

Today, when I talk to groups of people abroad, one statement always elicits spontaneous applause: We modified our gun regulations in ten days. Applause happens regularly. It actually happens every time I say those words. That answer demonstrates that even in places where gun violence appears intractable and reform is nearly impossible, people have not given up. They refuse to accept violent extremism as inevitable, or gun violence as the new normal.

But it also tells me something else: that every crisis calls for immediate and unequivocal action. And it'll keep asking. Until there is change.

Plus, there was the video issue. The shooter had live televised the incident on March 15, which lasted seventeen minutes before being stopped. For the first twenty-four hours, the film was shared on YouTube at a rate of one per second, while Facebook erased 1.5 million copies.

I even discovered the footage myself, shortly after the assault, when I opened Instagram to share information with the public. I was still in New Plymouth at the time, on my way to the airport, and the video's appearance on my feed had been so upsetting, so viscerally horrific, that I threw my phone on the floor of the van.

If I saw it, how many others did? How many still would? What impact would that have?

This video was prepared not only to revictimize individuals who were harmed and their families, but also to serve as a tool to incite both copycats and retribution acts. I would hear repeated reports from those who had witnessed it, including family members, friends, and members of the Muslim community. I couldn't conceive a world in which the worst thing that could happen to you—the murder of a loved one—was videotaped and broadcast to the entire globe.

In the days following the incident, social media giants like Facebook came out and requested a meeting. But I knew that if I met with them, they would most likely apologize, take a photo, and then leave. There was the possibility that nothing would change. For a little moment in time, we had the ability to request more.

I phoned Angela Merkel. Next came Emmanuel Macron and Justin Trudeau. I asked whether they would join New Zealand to make a bigger ask. When they agreed, I called Facebook's Mark Zuckerberg. I contacted Jack Dorsey from Twitter, Sundar Pichai from Google, Susan Wojcicki, the CEO of YouTube, Amazon's Jeff Bezos, and, most importantly, Brad Smith, the president of Microsoft, who was a strong supporter of our efforts. Within eight weeks, we created and published the Christchurch Call to Action, a pledge to eliminate terrorist and violent extremist content online.

As I write, governments, civic society, and big corporations—more than 130 in total—have joined the Christchurch Call. Because of this, the globe now has new crisis protocols, tools, and rules that did not exist before to the March 15 assaults. These include a worldwide crisis response system to prevent the spread of live-streamed assaults, limitations on live streaming implemented by digital platforms, and investments in new technologies to assist researchers in understanding the influence of algorithms and how people get radicalized online.

But violence breeds violence. And as long as that loop persists, both online and offline, the fight against violence must continue. No, the sadness of March 15 has not left me. But perhaps some sadness was never intended. Perhaps sadness can keep you focused on change.

CHAPTER 18

In the weeks following March 15, my mind occasionally wandered. Government business continued, occasionally with urgency. But that was fine. Keeping active allowed me to avoid spending too much time alone with my thoughts.

I had campaigned on the topic of a capital gains tax, which taxes profits on investments other than family residences. These profits were a significant source of income for our wealthiest individuals, and it seemed only reasonable to tax them in the same way that we taxed wage-based income. I believed in this transformation; it was about fairness, and Grant was especially invested. However, New Zealand First believed that a capital gains tax was overly cumbersome. As March turned into April, and then more weeks passed, I began to wonder if we'd be able to do anything.

At home, Neve and Clarke were my solace. Clarke would email me brief video of their day whenever I was gone from them for an extended period of time. The videos were easy. Neve in her Jolly Jumper, bouncing up and down in a doorway, sometimes with such force that I thought she was about to spring away from the frame entirely. Then there were her culinary escapades. She was 10 months old now, and each meal was a disaster. Smeared pumpkin and avocado, with chicken bits scattered across the kitchen floor. She was also starting to pull herself up, moving around the edge of the sofa, shaky but determined.

When I was at home, watching Neve discover new locations within her reach or remove every piece of Tupperware from the kitchen drawers, my thoughts drifted back to my own youth. All those small moments that made me happy: The aroma of fresh milk spilled over a cowshed pad. The feel of sun-warmed, freshly cut grass against my bare feet. Salt spray from a windswept beach. I craved most for the seashore.

So, a month after the terrorist incident, Clarke and I packed our car, strapped Neve into her car seat, and drove to the airport to fly to the east coast for the Easter holiday. Clarke's family owned a small fiberboard beach house (called a bach in New Zealand) at Māhia, a magnificent region with long, smooth expanses of golden sand, low dunes, and protected forest blanketing slopes overlooking the lake.

I enjoyed spending time with Clarke's folks. They were doers. His father, Tony, was an orchardist. Now retired, he wandered around his farm like a happier version of my grandfather Eric. When we visited, I'd wake up in the morning to find him already outside, erecting stakes for bean plants or organizing his tools. While at the beach, Tony discovered a particularly lovely plank of wood that had washed up. He dragged it home and within a few days had transformed it into a completely functional coffee table. Clarke's mother, Peri, was a social worker who had previously run a floral business called Peri's Tropicana. She could also knit, crochet, and reupholster. Clarke was five when he was cast as "the lonely little Petunia" in a school musical. Peri had designed his costume, carefully avoiding the calamity that had befallen the other children in the onion patch when one fainted because the stocking on his head was too tight.

Peri and Tony had previous experience with grandparenting; Neve was their sixth granddaughter. When visitors arrived, they were greeted by a chest full of storybooks, dolls, and tea sets, many of which were from Clarke and his sisters' childhood. Tony was the type of guy who would stop what he was doing to chase the kids around, whereas Peri would get down on the floor to do a puzzle, read a book, or create a fairy garden.

They were also always willing to babysit so Clarke and I could walk down the beach or enjoy Clarke's favorite hobby, watching boats launch at Mokotahi Beach. Clarke and I were never truly alone on these outings, of course. As prime minister, I always had my diplomatic protection team around, but after nearly a year and a half, we'd grown accustomed to these silent, round-the-clock shadows.

Clarke and I went on one such hike during the Easter 2019 holiday: up Mokotahi Hill, a short, steep climb that led to a stunning view of Taylor's Bay. I wasn't really in the mood for a walk that day; I was exhausted and deflated. Not only was I still suffering from March 15, but I had also discovered that Winston Peters and New Zealand First would oppose the implementation of a capital gains tax. That means we didn't have enough numbers to make it. So, shortly before the break, I took a strategic decision to take it off the table for the next election. I was concerned that if we campaigned on a capital gains tax for the fourth election in a row, New Zealand We might try to nix it again, risking losing votes to them in the process. I knew I had disappointed many, particularly Grant, and that I had left a major issue in our tax system unaddressed.

I didn't want to trek, nor did I want to talk about the terrible week we had just had. But I saw Clarke was excited to walk the hill, so I decided to accompany him. The hike would be strenuous, but it was short enough that we could return before Neve's dinnertime. But when I saw Clarke loading water bottles into a backpack, I worried if he planned to trek more than simply the hill.

"Come on!" he exclaimed, already outside the door. I sighed, tied my shoelaces, and followed Clarke, our on-duty DPS officer, with Iain following closely after. Iain, like all DPS agents, was stoic and alert. Unlike others, he did not blend into the crowd. He was rather tall, for starters, but it was his shaved head and strong beard—a "magnificent beard," as some on social media had described it—that earned him the label #hipsterbodyguard.

The trail was small, making it impossible for Clarke and me to walk side by side. He took the lead, going a little too quickly up the incline, while I dragged behind, attempting to keep up. Although it had been ten months after Neve's arrival, I was still struggling to regain some of my fitness. As I puffed up the hill, Iain pretended he wasn't walking at a snail's pace behind me.

When we reached the ridge, Clarke sat in the long grass. I sat down next to him, pulling in breath and attempting to reduce my heart rate. I felt ancient, and I realized I looked it too, dressed in Lycra tights, a sweatshirt, and Clarke's Honda Marine helmet. This is what I was wearing when Clarke approached me and asked me to marry him.

Clarke has always astonished me. He wasn't into elaborate romantic acts or red roses and jewels. Instead, dad slipped handwritten messages under my pillow whenever he traveled. When we flew back from New York, he wrote a note on a napkin expressing how proud he was of me and put it onto my fold-down tray while I was in the bathroom. There were so many instances like that.

There was the cup of tea, lovingly placed by my bedside to help me face the day—not only on occasion, but every morning without fail—and the one at the end of the night after he had done the dishes. When I returned home, Dad always seemed to know whether it was a day to rant, drift over, or chuckle. And if it was one for laughing, he would make sure we both laughed so hard that we forgot about everything else in the world. These were the continuous actions of someone who did not simply make my life simpler. Clarke made my life better.

So, will I marry him? Yes. A heartbeat.

Clarke took out of his rucksack a small bottle of Lindauer, a surprisingly good low-cost New Zealand sparkling wine, and a huge chocolate Easter egg wrapped in gold foil. I felt a hard thing knock against the interior. Clarke's grandmother's ring, a 1920s art-deco band with two square diamonds in the center, was mysteriously hidden within the chocolate egg. We sat in the vast grass for a little while after he slid it on my finger. Iain paced nearby, keeping an eye out for anyone approaching the route.

"Do you think he noticed?" I inquired. That was a joke. DPS were quiet witnesses to all key life events.

"Nah," Clarke replied. We joked and drank wine from disposable cups. Taylor's Bay, below us, was covered with driftwood. During my first visit to Māhia, Clarke launched a dinghy and showed me his childhood fishing sites as we discussed my campaign objectives. And now we'd added another memory to this treasured site.

When we arrived home, Neve was in her high chair, and Peri was feeding her. Peri looked up eagerly and gave a knowing laugh. Of course, I thought. Who else could have expertly placed the ring inside the Easter egg except Peri? She hugged me and we sat at the table as she recounted finding the antique, a ring belonging to Tony's mother, in its hiding place.

While we spoke and joked, Clarke made faces at Neve. She grinned and giggled as he lifted her up and walked her to the washtub. I took it all in: the sun beaming across the room, the sound of the splashing down the hall, and Peri talking to me. I counted myself very lucky.

A week following his engagement, Prince William, Duke of Cambridge, traveled to New Zealand to meet the March 15 victims. I met Prince William for the first time at the opening of our new Supreme Court building; the governor-general had invited me to a Pacific-themed BBQ for the prince and young leaders. As a new MP, I was really apprehensive in my bright floral dress, half hiding behind one of the enormous native trees strewn around the governor-general's back garden. The prince strolled among the guests, genuinely interested in who they were and what they had to say.

He eventually neared our group, and my tree was no longer providing cover. While I didn't know what to say, another MP, Darren Hughes, stepped in. The prince visited Kāpiti Island, a popular nature reserve and bird sanctuary within Darren's electorate. Darren asked Prince William how he appreciated the visit and related a moment as an MP visiting Kāpiti when he held out his arms and birds landed on him en masse.

I chuckled, nearly forgetting about our company, and asked Darren whether it was also "a scene from Ace Ventura: Pet Detective." Even as the words left my mouth, I thought, You did not just say that. Prince William, however, chuckled, saying a bird had also fallen on him. Or maybe he was only being courteous. Anyway, I retired behind my tree. My second experience with him was not much better. In 2014, Prince William and the Duchess of Cambridge visited New Zealand again, this time with baby George. There was a lot of excitement and hype, and many people wanted to see the couple, so an event was organized specifically for MPs and their guests. To help the royal couple move through the crowd more swiftly, everyone was divided into groups of eight, with one person in each group in charge of introduction. Crystal, my cousin, was my plus one. She was a huge royal enthusiast who collected memorabilia and even hosted a themed party to commemorate the couple's engagement.

The duchess looked stunning that evening when she entered the room and approached our group first. She wore a black fitting dress with a platinum- and diamond-encrusted fern brooch, which was given to Queen Elizabeth on her 1953 visit to New Zealand. David Shearer, the former Labour leader, greeted her and led her to where my cousin and I were nervously standing. I stood bolt upright, as if I were undergoing a military examination.

"This is Jacinda Ardern," David declared, and I smiled.

His arm extended to my cousin. "And this is her partner, Crystal," remarked the gentleman. We glanced at each other with our mouths half open. I had planned a greeting, but David's introduction threw me off, and the duchess had already gone on.

Crystal muttered, "Did he just say we were…together?"

"I think so," I answered.

"Should we tell her we're cousins?" Crystal inquired. We had a brief discussion and determined that the chance of confusion—that we were both in a relationship and cousins—was probably too great.

David Shearer started leading the duchess to the next group. Before leaving, she leaned down to say, "You both look beautiful." Then she was gone.

I hoped this royal visit would be different. I was still concerned about my tendency to say the incorrect thing, but I wasn't a "guest" any longer. My objective was to inform Prince William, the heir to the throne and someone with a strong interest in New Zealand, about what happened on March 15. I had a very specific plan in mind: I would introduce the prince to the Muslim community and then stand aside.

We first went to Starship Children's Hospital in Auckland to see one of the youngest victims of the attack: a five-year-old girl whose father and mother had kept vigil over her bed while she lay in a coma. She had awoken, and seeing her now, propped up in bed, talking with the prince, was like seeing a miracle.

I noticed how the prince bent down when he spoke with youngsters in the hospital, looked them in the eyes, and asked questions that only a parent with small children would know to ask. Over the years, I'd seen a number of politicians and prominent personalities connect with people. You could always tell when someone was simply going through the motions. When the prince asked questions, he listened carefully to the responses, his look that of someone who had experienced loss. It dawned to me that he must have been jet-lagged following the exhausting twenty-four hours of flight from England. He probably missed his family too. But he never exhibited any of this.

That afternoon, we traveled to Christchurch. Over the roar of the engines, we talked about rugby and his trip to New Zealand, and his fascination with helicopters and my phobia of them. We also discussed the attack and what I had learned about some of the families he would visit the next day. By the time we landed, I'd told him about Neve, and Clarke and my engagement, which we hadn't yet publicly publicized.

Two days later, the prince returned to London. During his brief visit, the media asked the same question they always did when I spoke with the royal family. I believed that New Zealand should eventually become a republic with its own head of state. Did this make the visit awkward? It hadn't. Neither had my opinion changed. But one thing did.

I had always admired the royal family, but witnessing what they did up close was something else. As I sat with Prince William on that plane flight, it seemed to me that his time in public office, unlike mine, was for life. Most New Zealanders will recall photographs from Prince William's first visit to the nation with his parents. He'd been 10 months old at the time, the same age as Neve now, and he'd been sitting on the Government House lawn in a romper, playing with a Buzzy Bee, an iconic New Zealand toy. He had been in front of the cameras.

I had entered public life at the age of twenty-eight, and my position would inevitably come to an end. A new prime minister would be appointed, followed by another. I would move on to other things and live a tranquil life. He never would. I wondered what it would be like to know that your duties would never stop. Despite this, I never saw any arrogance or animosity against his life. Not at a barbecue, at a hospital, or on a flight. I was unsure how he accomplished it.

A few weeks later, after a student journalist discovered my engagement ring and I eventually announced publicly that Clarke and I were getting married, a beautiful bouquet of flowers arrived at the Beehive to congratulate me and Clarke on our engagement. William and Catherine signed it.

Many additional people, including dignitaries, diplomats, and leaders, visited New Zealand to pay their condolences to the Muslim community. Russell M. Nelson, the president of the Church of Jesus Christ of Latter-day Saints—or the Mormon prophet, as he was often known—paid me arguably the most unexpected visit.

Nelson traveled to New Zealand to express sorrow on behalf of all church members and offer a $100,000 payment to help restore the damaged mosques. My team and I had begun working to bring together leaders from many faith traditions to address topics ranging from safety and security to how we could foster greater cross-faith understanding.

As a child, I was curious about my classmates' families' beliefs—why one attended church on Saturday while another did not celebrate Christmas. Sometimes my curiosity got the best of me, like when I asked a religious teacher if the Immaculate Conception meant Jesus was adopted. However, studying about diverse faiths taught me that understanding one another's religions may help me learn more about individuals. I believe that youngsters are inherently interested and welcoming. So, what would our world be like if, as adults, we met others with the inclusiveness we were born with, rather than the exclusion we were taught?

I knew a little about President Russell Nelson, at least on paper. I learned he was a retired heart surgeon, ninety-four years old, and had held church seniority for more than thirty years. In contrast, I was a lapsed Mormon and unmarried mother who openly celebrated our LGBTQ+ community, voted for marriage equality, worked to alter abortion laws, and believed that conversion therapy should be banned. I wasn't sure how the meeting would proceed.

President Nelson came unaccompanied into my ninth-floor office. His movement and spirit belied his age of nine and a half decades. He had a traditional air about him—he wore a sober suit with a striped tie and polished shoes—but he also exuded warmth. He had laugh lines around his eyes and leaned in to where I sat at my conference room table. When he spoke, he did it quietly, hands clasped, his tone a mix of gravitas and humility. He was kind. Absolutely nonjudgmental. Just like the church members and missionaries I'd known my entire life. Just as my parents had always been, even after I had left the religion that was so important to them.

I'd met a lot of people who had abandoned organized religion, including myself. Many of these stories featured heartbreak. Many had lost not only their entire neighborhood, but their family members. Sitting opposite President Nelson, I felt fortunate. I may have turned away from the church, but I never felt that anyone turned away from me. And here we were, the prophet and the former Mormon from Morrinsville, two very different individuals who had followed radically different paths and believed very different things, yet both hoped to bring a little more oneness into the world.

By June, Neve was standing on her own, rocking unsteadily as she attempted to figure out the difficult business of walking. My mother, who, along with Peri and my cousin Lynn, was an important part of our core child-care team while Clarke was filming, became concerned that I might miss Neve's first steps. She also tried to influence the process by urging Neve to keep the furniture for a little longer.

One day, Lynn texted me. Neve is attempting to walk, she wrote. Then she cheerfully added, "Maybe she'll do it this weekend when you get home!" When I saw Neve take uncomfortable steps a few days later, I couldn't help but wonder if I was watching an encore rather than an opening performance.

Neve's first word was, "Dad." This milestone was swiftly followed by other words, including "cheese," "hi," and "poo." But she didn't say

"Mum," or "Mumma." I tried my best to coach her. I occasionally whispered the word into her ear when she lay in her cot at night. "Mumma," I'd say, watching her smile back at me, her adorable pudgy fingers clawing at my face and pulling on my hair. "Say 'Mumma.'"

When I was feeding her breakfast in her high chair or giving her a bath, I would encourage her to replicate what I did. "Mumma. "Can you say 'Mumma'? I joked with Clarke about it: "She'll recite the alphabet before she says it."

One day, an old friend came. He recorded Neve as she played with an empty toilet paper roll. "Can you say hi?" my friend inquired.

"Hiiiii," Neve murmured, holding the roll firmly between her lips.

"Know what she can't say, though?" I asked, chuckling. "Mumma."

At that point, Neve set down the toilet paper roll. "Mumma," she stated. My father would shout on the All Blacks rugby team, so I flung my hands in the air as well. Not because she said it, but because I was present.

Foreign leaders sent Neve gifts on her first birthday, just as they did when she was born. South Korean President Moon sent her a traditional first birthday dress, complete with cap and little shoes. Prince William, who shares Neve's birthday, sent her a Buzzy Bee, the toy he was pictured playing with as a youngster when he visited New Zealand. But with a plaque on the bottom that reads, "Happy Birthday, Neve, from Prince William."

I decided that to make up for my absence, I would make Neve's birthday cake from scratch. My culinary quest would be guided by New Zealand's holy grail cookbook, the famed, iconic Australian Women's Weekly Children's Birthday Cake Book. This novel was well-known in New Zealand during the 1980s and 1990s.

It taught parents how to make more than 106 potential children's cakes: A three-dimensional boxcar steam engine train cake with connectable cars. An huge "rubber ducky" cake decorated with popcorn feathers and a bill made of two concave potato chips. Cakes in the shape of robots, or an aboveground swimming pool in which divers splash around in "water" composed of blue jelly held together by a tenuous ring of chocolate fingers.

I opted to go with one of the simpler options: a rabbit, which is nearly two-dimensional, and an ode to Neve's favorite cuddly bunny, Buddy. But I only started after I'd made a dent in my work briefcase. It was the early hours of the morning when I finally prepared and baked the cake, waited for it to cool, and began the dreaded icing "crumb coat," Clarke added gently, "Maybe you and I can take turns making her birthday cake, so you don't have to do this every year."

"Sure," I responded, pleased that next year he would be battling with the spatula.

Nobody had asked me to create a cake. Nobody even expected me to. If I had gone up to Neve's party with a store-bought cake or no cake at all, no one would have noticed. But, in my opinion, there was a bare minimum set of "Mum" tasks I needed to complete. And I'd be darned if an Australian Women's Weekly cake wasn't among them.

CHAPTER 19

Becoming a mother changed me. Not simply as an individual, but also as a politician. I didn't become more focused on children's policy; I had always been interested in it. But now I think of the strength of parents who raised their children on their own virtually every day, and the support they may require. I was confident that if we focused more on families' experiences as a whole, we could help children thrive.

We frequently asserted that New Zealand was the best place in the world to raise children. There was truth to this. We had free universal health care for children, a good education system, plus beaches, forests, and rural landscapes that made an ideal "backyard" for a youngster.

But I also wanted us to be the best environment in the world to raise a child. We weren't there yet. We had a housing problem, significant levels of child poverty, family violence, and a mental health system that was severely strained. Resolving these challenges would be neither straightforward nor quick. But, while I knew there would be no miracles, I also realized there would be no progress if we continued to believe that the old institutions were adequate.

Grant had long advocated for a shift away from basic economic measurements such as GDP—gross domestic product, the gold standard for assessing a country's prosperity. As our finance minister, the most crucial position in the cabinet outside of prime minister, Grant wanted to understand not only how much money was flowing through our economy, but also our country's overall health and well-being. Grant had previously mentioned that a business owner may be polluting our rivers while also dealing with family mental health concerns. However, as long as the business is profitable and pays taxes, GDP will declare everything is fine.

By mid-2019, we were finally able to create the budget we desired, one that looked beyond GDP as the sole measure of our well-being and indicator of where investment should be put. Under Grant's guidance, we created something called the Wellbeing Budget.

It wasn't simply a title. The initiatives that contributed the most to our national well-being were given priority in financial allocation. Among other things, this meant investing $1.9 billion over four years in mental health projects.

Mental health work has always felt personal. It had been over twenty-five years since I learnt that my friend Fiona's brother had committed suicide, and the memories of that time had never faded. In the years since, I've met a lot of folks who have either struggled or know someone who has.

Everyone knew somebody. And every story I heard, every mother who told me about losing a child to suicide, every person who told me about losing a brother, a parent, an uncle, or a friend, always took me back to that day, the helpless despair I'd felt and witnessed when one of the brightest, cleverest kids I'd ever known was suddenly gone.

Officials pressured us. They pointed out that, along with the minister of health, I had accepted virtually all the remaining forty proposals. They stated it would be noticeable if I didn't accept this, too. But I could not. The idea of standing in front of a bereaved family and telling them that as long as there were fewer suicides, we would have achieved our aim seemed terrible.

"If not 20%, what is the target? "An adviser pressed me. "Do we have one? "

I did. I knew this goal would be attacked and condemned as unreasonable and unreachable. It signified unavoidable failure. Any other figure, however, would indicate to the public that we were willing to tolerate disaster and loss. But I didn't.

"The target is zero," I stressed. The health minister agreed, and this is what we declared.

During our time in office, we would increase welfare payments for families with children, build more state housing than any government in the previous fifty years, expand access to early childhood education and health care, invest in violence prevention programs, and implement free period products in schools. However, we also wanted to feature children's perspectives.

When we began designing the plan, we asked the youngsters to share their hopes. Thousands of postcards were sent out, and in response, we received drawings, photographs, and handwritten remarks. I read each one as it came in. The strategy team framed several of these postcards, which I hung above the entrance to the Premier House flat so that I couldn't go home or leave for work without seeing them. Staying with your family. To be accepted. Be understood and taken seriously. If the parents are good, the children are excellent.

On the morning of the launch, while we were still in Premier House, I was packing the final few items into a diaper bag. A change of clothes in case of an accident on the plane, a bottle and formula for the flight (to aid Neve's ears), and nappies. I need to put in some additional nappies. Where did we leave Buddy the Bunny? There will be no peace if I forget Buddy.

Her head slumped backwards, and her body began to shake. Mum had a seizure. This had happened before, but the physicians had never figured out why. Eventually, they attributed it to dehydration and heat. But hearing my father's description of the seizure was one thing. Another thing I noticed about her was the absent expression in her eye and the way her body trembled.

"Brad!" I said urgently. But Brad was already there, lowering Mum's seat as far as it could go and signaling to the flight attendant for an oxygen tank.

Mum was no longer shaking when the plane descended into Auckland. She had vomited and hyperventilated, but she could now breathe normally. Mum persisted, "I'm fine," even as she was loaded into a wheelchair. "It has happened before." I will be alright!"

She'd be alright, as it turned out. Experts concluded the seizure was likely caused by a virus. However, I was unaware of this at the time. Meanwhile, my mother was being hospitalized. Neve was in my arms. Hundreds waited for me in Rotorua. I had no notion where I was meant to go right now.

I texted rapidly, attempting to come up with a plan. My cousin Lynn may meet my mother at the hospital. My sister was home with her son, and she could care for Neve as long as I could get her to her. But my flight to Rotorua was ready to depart. Should I simply cancel the event? The scenarios went through my mind. If I didn't show up, there would be questions. Why was I not there? Would journalists approach my mother in the hospital? I was saddened by the notion of disappointing the students at school. Every option was horrible.

Another DPS officer, Taff, offered to take Neve to my sister's house in the van we had reserved for my mother and Neve. I knew Taff well. He was a happy dad. But could I really drop her in a vehicle with a DPS officer? I started buckling Neve into the car seat before I knew what I was going to do. I realized then that the role of a DPS officer could have been to blend in and keep me safe from threats or violence. They had, however, witnessed me laughing, playing with my child, cursing, and even crying. There were countless times when I could have felt alone—in the back of a car, walking to work, moaning about a poor phone conversation or press conference—but I wasn't. People's surrounded me 24 hours a day, seven days a week. They'd gotten to know me, and it appeared they'd also gotten to know my daughter.

They closed the van door and left. I gulped hard, turned around, and dashed for my plane.

Mum was fine and on her way to being discharged when I arrived in Rotorua. Neve was fine, too. But I was sidetracked, repeating the morning in my mind. Had I made the right decision continuing my day? Was that the wrong one? I flipped back and forth.

Then we entered the school hall, which was filled of intermediate-aged pupils. There were probably hundred of them in the chilly afternoon breeze. The children exploded into an exuberant rendition of the haka. Their eyes were big, and their voices were forceful. Near the front row, one of the kids—a boy with a buzz cut, maybe no more than ten years old, lean legs poking through his shorts—looked directly at me as he moved. His performance was intense. The kids around him were doing an excellent job with the haka. But this youngster was feeling it.

I realized I needed to take these questions seriously. In adjoining rooms, I saw folks proving their jousting abilities.

No, I marked the form. I couldn't joust. But I did know how to ride bareback, a talent I learned as a child while assisting a neighbor, Mrs. Bonner, with her ponies, Prince and Princess.

Unfortunately, I was not one of the half-million New Zealanders who appeared in The Lord of the Rings. However, my botched venture into Peter Jackson's trilogy served as a wonderful discussion starter when Stephen Colbert, a Lord of the Rings fan, visited New Zealand to explore the set of his favorite film.

Colbert's visit to New Zealand sparked widespread excitement. It was an opportunity to promote New Zealand tourism, a multibillion-dollar sector, which I was delighted to be a part of. That's perhaps why I didn't fully evaluate all of the hazards involved in a seemingly simple request: "Can you pick Stephen up from the airport?" "

I still drove myself all the time. I also did occasional airport runs. So another thirty-minute journey didn't seem like a huge problem, even if cameras would be rolling. Sure, he made a little dent in the back of my car as he enthusiastically flung his bags into the trunk. And he tried to unlock my phone so many times by guessing the passcode that it eventually disabled itself. But he was so entertaining that by the end of the drive, my stomach hurt from laughing so hard. That was until Stephen Colbert used the term "sing-along."

I couldn't sing. I'd known I couldn't sing since intermediate school, when my teacher Miss Barr forced me to perform "Old MacDonald Had a Farm" in front of my classmates in the school hall, and after one verse, announced definitely that I couldn't sing.

New Zealand is commonly called the "shaky isles" due to its seismic activity. Its terrain is peppered with volcanic cones. Our lengthy history of natural calamities requires us to be prepared. We grow up performing earthquake drills, and in government, you never know when you'll need to respond to a catastrophic event. Despite our combined preparation and resilience, each incident leaves a scar.

On Monday, December 9, 2019, I emerged from a weekly cabinet meeting to discover that Whakaari/White Island, an active volcano and popular tourist destination in the Bay of Plenty, had erupted, spewing volcanic gasses, boulders, and ash into the air. When it happened, 47 people, largely visitors and guides, were on the island, which is effectively the volcano's summit. Several people had been saved, but the local hospital was swamped by severe burn injuries. Up to 27 people remain missing. While it was assumed that none of those still on the island had survived, the poisonous circumstances and risk of future eruptions made further recovery nearly impossible.

As I took this in, my mind had one rapid idea. Enough. It faded as soon as it appeared, but it remained long enough for me to properly register it. Just nine months prior, we had witnessed a terrible domestic terror assault. We had also witnessed floods and wildfires. Now a volcano. It was the first time I realized that tragedies might just keep coming. A country does not receive a quota. There wasn't such thing as enough. It was life, and it was filled with unimaginable tragedy.

That night, I flew to Whakatāne with my press secretary Andrew, the minister of civil defense, and the head of Civil Defence Emergency Management. The scene on the ground was naturally chaotic. Cruise ship operators were attempting to reconcile lists of who had left their ships that day to tour Whakaari, who had been accounted for, and who had not.

Over the next several days, agencies attempted to devise a plan to return to the island. My chief science adviser, Juliet Gerrard, collaborated with volcanologists to determine the likelihood of future activity. A navy vessel was eventually stationed nearby, and young men and women who were often deployed for bomb disposal operations donned heavy safety gear, climbed onto inflatable boats, and began a laborious recovery task.

When you are close to situations involving pain and loss, such as March 15 or Whakaari/White Island, you understand how deeply personal and unique each individual's experience is. In the days following the eruption, I frequently thought of my aunty Marie and her own burn scars. She had been in and out of the hospital and undergone scores of surgeries throughout her adult life, and the memory of her injuries still made her shiver whenever she heard the sound of an ambulance. In the days following the eruption, as I visited and spoke with survivors and families of those who perished, I met people who were embarking on a lifelong journey of loss, healing, or, in many cases, both. I was just there for a little moment, at the beginnings of a tale that they will always be able to tell.

A day after the eruption, first responders and chopper pilots who helped with the rescue gathered in a nearby town center. I attended the function to thank them. Some of those present had participated in the most heroic acts imaginable and had suffered severe injuries. Just before I arrived, one of my employees showed me a post opposing my coming. They stated I was in Whakatāne to be photographed "hugging people." The post made me uncomfortable.

Primarily, of course I had left. This was a big calamity for our country, and I was Prime Minister. And scolding me for hugging others? Who had just gone through something as horrifying as they had? People had come to expect very little from politicians. I alternated between thinking this remark was extremely cynical and thinking it was simply sad.

It reminded me of something I'd always believed. My role entailed more than just responding to and providing resources for national catastrophes. I instinctively reached out and placed my hands on her shoulders. But, in turn, she wrapped her arms around me. I could hear the cameras click.

I knew this would simply feed my opponents, those who were skeptical of empathy and believed that everything was a performance. That's okay, I thought as I hugged her tightly in return. I'd rather be criticized than quit being human.

When the government closed for the Christmas break a few weeks later, we packed up the house and returned to the east coast to spend the holidays with Clarke's family.

On the first beautiful morning, we took Neve to the water. I dressed her in a rash shirt, a wide-brimmed hat to protect her thin golden hair, and applied thick white sunscreen on her nose as she crinkled her face at me. I spread a cloth and sat down. Then I observed Clarke take

Neve's hand and slowly guide her toward the calm ocean. Neve was now a toddler, so small that Clarke stooped awkwardly as she walked barefoot, pausing to pick up a shell or put her hands into the sand. When they got to the lake, they took slow steps. Neve squeezed her fists in horror at the cold. After adjusting to the water, she began fluttering her arms and squealing with glee. Clarke stood behind her, near enough to grasp her, hands on his waist as he followed her into the ankle-deep water and then out again. Over and over.

As I watched them, I began to imagine the scene going forward in time, with Neve becoming somewhat taller. Her hair grew longer, and her waddle turned into a walk. Then a run. Floaties transform into a boogie board, as Clarke no longer lifts Neve up and down over waves, but rather runs into them alongside her. I could picture everything, including the passage of time. The rapidity with which it came made me want to stop everything and push pause. Capture this moment in time.

To slow things down, I lifted my face into the sunlight and inhaled the salty air. My mind, the day, and time itself. 2019 was over. A new one was about to start.

CHAPTER 20

It was October 2021, more than eighteen months after COVID had arrived on our shores. I stood in the small nook that separates my Premier House bedroom and bathroom. A giant mirror with a tarnished gold frame hung on the wall in front of me, similar to one your grandmother may have in her spare room. There were a few waist-high shelves beneath the mirror, most of which held books I had been intending to read. This is where I kept my earrings: some in a peach jewelry container from Kmart, some in a wooden engraved box. I reached for the box now, reflecting on the country's—and my own—dilemma. An incarcerated individual carved the box as part of one of the initiatives we started in a New Zealand jail. It was carved from honey-colored rimu, a natural wood. The top of the box had a darker wood inlay with a stylized depiction of a rose in bloom, petals unraveling from around the rose's bud, and a long stem stretching out the length of the box.

I glanced at the box, wondering, "What are we going to do?"

Until now, we had kept COVID from spreading throughout New Zealand. But this time, the technique didn't work. We now had an outbreak of a variety known as Delta, which was not only more harmful than the initial strain, but also far more infectious. We were now having trouble tracing rough sleepers and gangs in areas. That meant Auckland and Northland were under a level 3 lockdown for the seventh week in a row, the longest we'd ever had.

Vaccines could help. We were actively getting them out, but it would be some time before we had enough people vaccinated to avoid serious disease and deaths. Meanwhile, I became increasingly convinced that we would not be able to eradicate COVID this time around. I also understood that everyone was fatigued, and New Zealand's feeling of community had begun to deteriorate. Many people were fed up with the continual interruptions in their lives and were becoming angry. Others remained terrified of COVID.

Again, I was presented with a difficult decision. Should I tell the nation what I believed to be true, that we might not be able to eradicate COVID this time? If I did, experts informed me, people would most likely give up and the spread would worsen. It might also incite rage and hostility toward the communities where COVID had taken hold.

Or should I say we were moving forward? Making modest modifications to ease constraints, because these changes will help individuals keep going. If I did that, people might not understand the changes. Everything felt like a "pick a path" book, where one option resulted in a firepit of doom and the other in suffocating quicksand, with the chance of ending up with both.

I made a decision: we would progressively loosen constraints, making minor improvements to make it easier to keep people going. I said, "Stay with it." However, it seemed more unlikely that we would succeed this time. The most we could do now was to slow the spread, reduce Delta's influence, and vaccinate as many people as possible.

My face seemed drawn. There was little I could do about it. I put on some lipstick and stepped out the door, towards the Beehive and the press conference.

On January 29, 2022, 14,000 kilometers from New Zealand, hundreds of trucks formed a convoy and descended on government buildings in Ottawa, Canada. According to the members of the "Freedom Convoy," the protest was sparked by the requirement for trucks crossing the United States border to be vaccinated.

Ten days later, a similar caravan of automobiles and demonstrators arrived on the forecourt of the New Zealand Parliament. By then, lockdowns had ended. persons claiming to lead the convoy stated that they were there due to "mandates," a government obligation that persons in specific frontline occupations, such as those working with the vulnerable—health care professionals or teachers—vaccinate. However, the signs raised by those on the forecourt revealed that their dissatisfaction was not limited to the mandates. Many people looked skeptical of immunizations as a whole. Others appeared to have issues with masks, the media, the UN, communism, and the government.

Protests are generally welcome in Parliament. When there is one, we supply power, speakers, and waist-high fencing to keep everyone safe. MPs will make daily visits to people gathered on the forecourt. Some MPs, including myself, have spoken at protests.

However, at all other marches, the demonstrators eventually returned home.

The first night, about a hundred individuals camped on Parliament grounds. Over the next three weeks, around 3,000 people would occupy either the grounds of Parliament or the neighboring streets. Some demonstrated peacefully, but others targeted businesses and locals. They blocked roads and set up makeshift toilets. Several commuters had their masks removed.

Early in the occupation, Trevor Mallard, who as speaker was officially in command of the Parliament grounds, set up speakers on balconies facing the forecourt and played Barry Manilow and subsequently the "Baby Shark" song on loop. Someone else—I'm not sure who—turned on the legislative sprinklers.

The occupation didn't end.

Each morning, I would come at my office, gaze out the window, and see what had happened the night before: whether the police had moved the barriers or whether there were any new areas of the grounds where tents had been set up. Showers were soon installed. It was like watching a village develop in real time.

The energy in the crowd fluctuated between a festival-like mood and a state of barely restrained wrath. I heard protest speeches and saw the signs. I saw my own image, complete with Hitler mustache, monocle, and the words "Dictator of the Year" above my face. I saw the gallows, replete with a noose, that people claimed had been erected for me. I saw American flags, Trump flags, and swastikas. At one point, I noticed the glint of literal tinfoil hats that some people had begun to wear, convinced that their headaches and flu-like symptoms were caused by electromagnetic fields emitted by the government rather than the current wave of COVID in New Zealand.

In my life, I've been a Mormon amid non-Mormons, a progressive among conservatives, and a woman in a predominantly male setting. Whatever the situation, I was always able to talk, debate, and disagree. To be a human first, then a leader. I realized now that to the rabble occupying Parliament, I was neither.

Protesters requested to speak with lawmakers. Only one MP, David Seymour from the ACT party, did. I refused. How could I convey the notion that if you disagree with anything, you may illegally seize the grounds of Parliament and get your requests fulfilled? No, I would not meet protesters. But I'd take a lesson from them.

While the occupation was focused on vaccines and regulations, some saw it as more. It was about trust, or rather mistrust. What appeared during the occupation was also larger than New Zealand. It was a global challenge—people could no longer agree on what was fact and what was fiction. People in the same areas or towns were experiencing distinct realities, which made fixing our problems even more difficult. As I looked out over Parliament's grounds, I was confident that we could only address this problem together on a global scale.

After twenty-three days, the police began an operation to relocate the occupation. Two hundred and fifty arrests were made, with forty officers injured. In the dying hours, demonstrators set fire to the Parliament playground, a popular spot for Wellington toddlers and schoolchildren. Dark smoke plumes billowed between pōhutukawa trees and Norfolk Island pines that had survived for over a century. White camellia-lined gardens commemorating our suffrage movement were trampled. Bricks were removed from the ground and converted into missiles.

Whatever drew the demonstrators to Parliament, it was evident by the end that it was no longer a place or institution in which they believed. I still think about this time a lot—not only the occupation, but the two years before it, with the long days and terrible choices. And, yeah, I do think about regret.

That word, "regret," conveys so much certainty. Regret means you know exactly what you would have done differently and the consequences of doing so. But we don't get to observe the counterfactual, the outcome of the decisions we didn't take. The lives that could have been lost. One thing is certain: I would have preferred different outcomes. I see a world where we save lives and bring everyone. Perhaps this is the distinction between regret and remorse.

But when I think of that moment, I also remember this: We emerged from COVID with one of the highest immunization rates in the world and less days in lockdown than countries such as the United Kingdom, and our country's life expectancy actually increased.

So when someone approaches me to tell me that they thought all of our decisions were wrong, perhaps in a less polite manner, perhaps with fists raised and their face twisted with fury, or in an expletive-filled rant, I remember that all of those difficult, imperfect decisions saved twenty thousand lives. And the person in front of me might be one of them.

CHAPTER 21

In early 2022, I returned to Premier House alone. We had spent a significant portion of our vacation in Gisborne, at Peri and Tony's property, where we spent our days gazing out at the sea, making sandcastles, breaking sandcastles, and leaping over waves. At three and a half years old, Neve was enthralled with wave jumping with her father; she grasped Clarke's hands, and he lifted her above every incoming swell.

"Again and again! " she cried, making Clarke's arms throb and tremble in the cold.

Clarke and I sat in his parents' bay window in the evenings, holding spools of fishing line while Clarke coiled it into reels to catch kingfish and snapper. I liked completing tiny repetitive tasks together.

As summer came to a conclusion, Clarke and Neve planned to continue in Gisborne for another week or so. But Parliament was about to reconvene, so I returned.

I dropped my bag and turned. Then I headed to Kmart.

Later that night, a friend and I removed the dark furniture, wrapped up the old Persian rugs, stored useless computer displays in the office, and transported a gray-glass TV cabinet from the lounge to the landing.

Instead, we built flat-pack furniture: a plain oak-veneer TV stand and a simple side table with long white metal legs. A white cubic bookcase, a little wooden table and chairs, and a vibrant pink bedside table for Neve. We put down a beige-and-white cotton floor covering and navy blue pillows on the old cream leather sofa. I discovered a few art pieces in storage and displayed them in the lounge and on the office walls.

None of this was elaborate or really fashionable. It was utilitarian, as you'd expect from a big-box retailer. But I wasn't looking to win any interior design competitions. I really wanted the area to feel different—lighter and more like it belonged to us.

When Neve arrived at Premier House a few days later, she dashed in as quickly as her little legs could carry her. I wondered why she seemed taller when I had only been away from her for a few days. She was looking less like a toddler and more like a youngster. She paused at the top of the stairs, just before reaching her bedroom, and gasped when she spotted her new table.

"A place to craft! She exclaimed enthusiastically. Crafting was her favorite pleasure. She could spend hours at the old coffee table we had adapted, breaking up cereal boxes, embellishing them with crayons, cotton, or shells, and covering everything with adhesive tape.

One night, about this time, I returned from a long day at work and looked in on her. I assumed she was sleeping, but from her bed she mumbled, "Mummy?" "

"Yes, darling," I said, laying my briefcase down. "It's just me."

Neve sat in bed with her beloved animals stacked around her. In the corner beside her head was a purple embroidered cushion made for her by a stranger when she was born. All of those newborn presents were so kind, and it seemed incredible that they had come at our door several years ago. I sat on the edge of the bed, massaging Neve's back, attempting to encourage her back to sleep.

Neve rarely grumbled about my job, which surprised me. When she was born, I was afraid she would continually lament my absence. I expected her to equal my guilt with guilt-inducing remarks. It had not been. What I felt, that persistent need to be with her more, was entirely my own creation. But tonight, Neve finally asked me the question I knew she would ask: "Mummy, why do you have to work so much? " We had never told Neve that I was the Prime Minister. We hadn't obscured or explained my job. I wanted her to know me only as Mumma. Not long ago, when asked what Mum did for a career, Neve said, "eat chocolate," referring to the hoard of chocolates in a drawer in my desk that she enjoyed to search out when she visited me at the Beehive. But she was no longer asking me what I did. She asked me why.

"Well, my darling," I murmured, adjusting her pajamas over her back and covering her petite body with the duvet. "I have a very important job."

"Do you like looking after me? "

In the dark, a jar on her bedside table shone with fairy lights. Buddy, her cozy, who was now worn and motley, was snuggled under her arm, exactly where Clarke would have placed him after reading her a goodnight story. I could see the entire evening routine that I'd missed: Clarke's distinct voices for each character, Neve's brilliant grin, the way she'd giggled while he read and then begged for "one more story, Dadda," when he ended.

"Yes," I told her. "Like looking after you. That is my most crucial task. But I also look after other folks.

Neve nodded enthusiastically, happy with the response, unaware of her simple query, "Why do you have to work so much?" had gotten to the heart of my difficulty, and that of other parents. Our children are the most essential thing to us and our top focus. But the most basic measure of their affection and concern was time. I had done everything to show my love in every other way: affection, comfort, patience, and my never-ending desire to be present.

But time continued to deceive me.

Neve begged to play hide-and-seek on a Saturday morning a few months later. In the corridor, she began counting to five, quickly at first, then slowly. Her hands only partially covered her face, and as I dashed into the room, I noticed her eyes peering between her tiny fingers. I ducked behind an immense armchair that had long been upholstered in salmon and gold.

Before long, it was Neve's fourth birthday, and I was back to fussing over a cake. Clarke baked her cake the previous year, and it was a success. Neve had asked him for three distinct themes: Moana, Frozen, and Mickey Mouse. The request may have confused many parents, but not Clarke. He made a cake in the shape of an antique tube TV, complete with licorice antennas, a stand of chocolate fingers, and dials made of chopped "licorice logs." He coated it in white fondant icing and outlined the "screen" with licorice straps. He then spent hours placing a projector above the table, which he used to show visuals from Moana, Frozen, and Mickey Mouse cartoons onto fondant. The visuals filled the screen accurately, and the entire thing was controlled by a remote. It was, I must say, incredible: Neve literally "watched" her cake before eating it.

Now it was my turn. I created a red ladybug.

A few days following the birthday, we celebrated Matariki, the Māori New Year. In 2020, we recognized this celestial event as the first Māori public holiday. This was the first year we officially marked it. It was midwinter and freezing that evening when Clarke, Neve, and I gathered with other families wrapped in coats and scarves beneath shimmering constellations. I stood back and saw Clarke haul Neve onto his shoulders, just another father and daughter blending in with the crowd in the dark. There were so many people attending Matariki events, including sunrise prayers, school events, and sunset walks. I reflected on what this new holiday represented: generations of children who would learn about their native country's entire customs in a way that my generation never did.

That's also why, after one year in government, we made teaching New Zealand history in schools obligatory. Now, all of our young people, including those who did not have a Mr. Fountain in the front of their classroom, would learn about our past to better comprehend our present. This was and continues to be one of the policies I am most proud of. It was about nation-building, not just curriculum. Indigenous Māori shared New Zealand's unique language, cultural traditions, and values, including pōwhiri (welcoming newcomers) and manaakitanga (showing kindness, generosity, and concern for others). This was a grace that, in my opinion, could only be completely appreciated if everyone understood the often-brutal history that came before it. In other words, if we could assist people comprehend our own country, we might be able to fix our flaws along the way.

There were other prior failures that needed to be addressed by the government, and we began to work on those as well. We established a royal commission on the state's care of children. We explored the Pike River Mine, the site of an infamous lethal coal-mining tragedy in 2010, to gather evidence that would allow victims' families to bring those responsible accountable. We offered a public apology for the 1970s immigration strategy known as the "Dawn Raids," which comprised actions of targeted intimidation and discrimination against Pacific community members. We did these things not to revisit old wounds, but to learn from the past and prevent future suffering.

After the world's borders reopened, I resumed worldwide travel. In May 2022, I traveled to the United States with a trade mission, spoke at Harvard's commencement about violent extremism, and met with President Biden for the first time. He was welcoming and generous as we talked about everything from regional security to trade to the conflict in Ukraine.

A month later, I returned to Europe to officially recognize the end of both the U.K. and EU free trade agreements. When we began government, 50 percent of New Zealand's global exports were covered by a free trade agreement; by now, we had increased that figure to more than 73%.

I returned from that trip to repeated flooding events—the kind we used to call a "once-in-a-century event" but were now witnessing every year. These just reinforced my commitment to our climate plans.

There were also happy moments amidst a hectic schedule. Adrian Rurawhe was elected to replace Trevor Mallard as Speaker of Parliament after he retired. He became the country's second Māori speaker, and his parliamentary seat was filled by a woman on our party list. For the first time in New Zealand's history, Parliament was 50% female.

We commemorated this historic milestone with a photo; MPs from across the house filed into the ancient parliamentary library, where some of the first photographs of New Zealand's all-male Parliament were taken more than 120 years ago. I beamed as I stood in front of the photograph. I was the 99th woman to enter Parliament. Just fourteen years later, that figure had risen to 177.

Changes were occurring everywhere. Liz Truss had also become Prime Minister of the United Kingdom, succeeding Boris Johnson, who had replaced Theresa May. I was reading the BBC news one evening before going to bed when I came across a story about Truss' first official meeting with the Queen. In the portrait, the queen was dressed in pastel blue. One hand rested on a cane, while the other reached forward to shake the hand of the incoming prime minister. I zoomed in on the queen's hand. Her skin was pale with a patch of dark purple. That's my grandmother's hand, I thought, recalling how Grandma Margaret's hand looked when Eric caressed it soon before she died. I felt a pang of despair. Then I put down my phone and turned out the light.

A few hours later, I woke up with a start. Someone was in the doorway. A flashlight flashed in the room. I only saw a beam of light through the darkness, not the person holding it. I sat up, bewildered.

"Sorry, ma'am," said the voice. It was a uniformed police officer. "It is the Cabinet Secretary. She states she needs to talk to you.

I knew immediately. Queen Elizabeth II, our head of state, had died.

The queen, the matriarch whose reign had lasted over seventy years and witnessed so many world changes that it was difficult to understand. The queen, who was nothing like my own grandmother, but who always reminded me of my childhood, staring at the back of her Queen Elizabeth hairstyle while a corgi trotted by her side.

In the days that followed, we performed all of the ceremonial tasks: we lowered our flags to half-mast, hung black ribbons from the corner of the queen's portrait, opened condolence books in Parliament, and began planning for memorial ceremonies and the transition to our new head of state, King Charles. But within, I was reflecting on all of the interactions I'd had with Her Majesty. She had called once throughout COVID to check in. Her stoicism when I reached out to share our nation's sorrow over the death of her husband and life companion. But mostly, I remembered her candid counsel when I asked her, still pregnant, how she handled her exceptional and unwavering public service career while still being a mother and grandmother.

"Just get on with it," she had urged. And, for the most part, she had been correct—one foot in front of another. You simply get on with it. Before attending the Queen's burial and meeting our new head of state, King Charles, I got a physical. Soon, I'd be visiting Scott Base, New Zealand's Antarctic research outpost that hosts approximately 80 people throughout the summer season. Although we were only supposed to stay for three nights, traveling into and out of Antarctica was fraught with complications. You couldn't risk a medical emergency in such an unclear setting. As a result, we have the physical.

It was a thorough examination from head to toe, including a complete blood panel. This included a breast examination, which is how they discovered the lump.

Is there a lump? Surely it was nothing, I convinced myself as soon as I heard my doctor say it. But for some reason, my GP began speaking quickly. Too quick.

"I'm sorry; I believe that's something you'll need to look into. It's on the left side, no larger than a centimeter and yet pretty little. I'm afraid there's not much more I can say." She hesitated, a startling stillness filling the place where her words had been; then she continued again, "I'm so sorry."

Was she apologizing for finding it, or for the inconvenience? Regardless, while I lay there on a vinyl exam table, the paper sheet underneath me crackled, I found myself soothing her. It's great, I'm sure it is; these things are frequent, I understand. For the most part, I believed this to be true. It probably was fine. Probably. Maybe. But I was also practical. I have a family history of breast cancer, including a relative who died in her 30s. I knew I was at high risk.

So, was everything fine?

Following the exam, I returned to the office. I barely had a few moments until cabinet and my customary news conference. I went to the toilet to fix myself, ignoring my talk with the doctor. The light in the dark tiled room always made me look a little rough, but as I stood at the sink, brushing my hair, I appeared even more wrong than usual.

Surely, I looked the same as I did this morning, yesterday, and the day before, before my doctor spoke the word "lump."

Standing there with my hairbrush, I decided not to tell Clarke. Not yet. Not until I learned more. Why worry him? In fact, why worry myself? It was probably nothing. I just needed to not think about it. That's what I'll do, I just won't think about it.

In a few minutes I would head to cabinet, and I would not think about it. Then I would talk to reporters and not think. I would go home, and I would hug Neve, put her to bed, and I would tell Clarke about all the other parts of my day. Just not this. Because I wouldn't be thinking about it.

But even as I stood there, trying to put my world into neat little compartments, the worst thoughts snuck in. What if it was cancer? How would I manage that and this job? How could anyone juggle it all? Maybe I wouldn't be able to. Perhaps then I could leave.

Perhaps I could leave?

I stood still, my hand still holding the hairbrush over the top of my head. What did I mean, perhaps I could leave? Where did that thought come from? And what kind of place was I in, if I was seeing cancer not just as a devastating possibility but as a ticket out of office?

There was nothing especially out of the ordinary going on that would have made that thought cross my mind, but it still did. Of course I was tired, but isn't everyone in their forties? And sure, I had contemplated my exit from politics, usually over the summer when I thought about long-term plans and what the future might look like—but not like this. This time, the thought had landed suddenly and unexpectedly, and my mind had grabbed it like a life ring. Rather than dwell on it any longer, though, I put my hairbrush down, walked out of the bathroom, and got ready for cabinet. I'm just tired, I thought.

Within a week I would have a breast scan. With that scan, any concern over the lump being cancerous would be gone. The fear would recede almost immediately. But not, as it turned out, the thought that had appeared with my fear, those three words.

That thought—I could leave—would linger.

I was cold. Very cold. I could no longer feel the tips of my fingers, even with two layers of gloves and heat packs resting in the palms of my hands. The wooden floorboards creaked under my heavy boots as I walked around slowly, taking in every detail. Near the cookstove, socks hung on the line, and legs of ham dangled from the ceiling more than a hundred years after they'd been placed there. The shelter in which I now stood, Ernest Shackleton's hut at Cape Royds, was an icy museum, one that looked more or less exactly as it had on the day its occupants walked out the door and never returned.

I had read Shackleton since I was a girl. He'd become a hero of mine. My dad had first sparked my interest, and since then I'd read extensively about the explorer. Shackleton was known for two failed missions. The place I was standing now had been part of his Nimrod Expedition, in 1908, in which he'd tried to reach the geographic South Pole. With his party, he'd trekked some seventeen hundred miles through the ice on foot until they were within ninety-seven nautical miles of their goal, when the conditions deteriorated so dangerously that Shackleton had done the unthinkable. He'd turned back for home. Standing here in the hut, I imagined what it must have been like to leave the security of warmth and shelter, to put so much on the line, and to have gotten so close to your goal, only to turn back. But Shackleton and the men with him had survived.

Back in sunny Auckland, a place that now seemed like a different planet altogether, I still drank from a worn and chipped mug with a Shackleton quotation: "Optimism is true moral courage." That mug sat on a shelf not far from framed prints of Shackleton's Endurance Expedition—which had failed when his ship was trapped, then crushed by pack ice, and which his party had also survived.

I'd spent so much of my life thinking about courage, and endurance, and survival. Now standing where Shackleton himself had once stood, I imagined him taking a final look around—at the food stores, the bunks, the specimen jars, the kettle and pots and pans—and I lingered for a moment, my back to the photographer standing nearby. I didn't want him to see my face. It might have been numb, but I could still feel my tears forming.

"Step back just a little more," the photographer told me. So I did, peering out the window into a landscape of dark gray, forbidding stones. Pockets of white snow dotted the landscape, eventually forming a bulk, followed by an endless, scary sea of white and nothing. David Seymour was the head of ACT, a right-wing libertarian party. He was young and confident, the type of guy who had previously worked at a conservative think tank and now pretended to be the world's leader. He'd been relentlessly assaulting me since the day I took office, and he was the only MP to vote against banning military-style semiautomatic guns after March 15 and reject our zero-carbon policies. He was also the sole MP to meet with the protesters who had occupied the Parliament grounds for a month.

During question time, he appeared to be more concerned with making clips for his own social media following than with receiving genuine responses. And today, he used his questioning to launch a series of attacks, first asking when I would "show some leadership" by removing a minister whom he had unfairly targeted. He also intimated that our proposal to broaden hate speech prohibitions in the Human Rights Act to protect religion was an overreach. Finally, he used a question to insinuate that I was incapable of acknowledging mistakes or expressing regret. At this point, I'd grown frustrated. When I had finished answering all of his inquiries, I sat down, turned to Grant, and, muttering, addressed David Seymour by name.

"Are you sure that's what I called him?" I questioned Andrew.

"The media heard it," Andrew stated, his expression serious. Then I went back and listened. You obviously referred to him as an arrogant prick."

I exhaled with a breath of relief. "Thank goodness," I replied. Andrew waited, puzzled. "I thought I called him a fucking prick."

I tried everything I could to mitigate the consequences. I openly apologized for the name-calling, using the old saying "If you don't have anything nice to say." David accepted my apologies, and we both signed a written transcript of the conversation, which was auctioned off for more than $100,000, with the proceeds benefiting the Prostate Cancer Foundation.

That probably should have been the end of the storyline. But I lingered on it. All these years, I'd done my best not to let the opposition get to me. However, I had recently noticed that things were bothering me more than usual. And it wasn't limited to the Beehive.

A month ago, during a news conference with Finland's Prime Minister Sanna Marin, I became irritated with a journalist. We had just concluded our meeting and were accepting questions when a New Zealand journalist raised his hand.

"A lot of people will be wondering," he told me, "are you two meeting just because you're similar in age and got a lot of common stuff there?" The connotation was plain. We weren't meeting because we were two prime ministers, but because we were girls.

I interrupted the journalist, asking aloud if anyone had questioned Barack Obama and John Key, New Zealand's previous prime minister, "if they met because they were of similar age." As I said the words, I could feel my anger rising. When we got off the podium, I felt compelled to apologize to Sanna.

"Don't worry," she added, chuckling. "But I do wish I had told him that instead of talking trade, we braided each other's hair."

Later that night, Clarke messaged me with some internet criticism around the press conference. It sounded like the journalist who had posed the question was being confronted. Sure, he should have known better than to ask such a question, but he was young and likely inexperienced, and he was now bearing the full brunt of the online community's criticism. Had I prepared the groundwork for his attack? Was I being less patient than I once was?

It wasn't the first time I'd encountered questions like this. In my early days as Labour leader, I chastised the journalist who argued that women should have to declare their reproductive plans. But then I felt like I was fighting for all women. Now I wondered if I was only fighting for myself.

But if I was losing patience, apparently others were, too.

I was at Auckland Airport, waiting for a commercial flight after a long day. Two staff members were accompanying me, but I separated from them to use the bathroom. I was standing at the basin, washing my hands, when a woman entered. She was around fifty years old and wore a bright blue stretch top with a lot of jewelry. She spotted me at the basin, almost as if she knew I'd be there, and proceeded deliberately toward me.

This was not rare. Even when I was a backbench MP, members of the public frequently contacted me at the supermarket or shopping mall. Since becoming Prime Minister, it has become a daily occurrence. It was the selfie age, and people frequently requested selfies—I'd even taken photos in front of restroom stalls. Other times, people wanted to talk about a specific issue—for example, the "civilianization" of the Defence Force, which one person mentioned as I was standing in a grocery store aisle deciding between muesli bars. Sometimes individuals merely wanted to say they saw me going about my business. at the early days of my prime ministership, just after announcing my pregnancy, I stood at Kmart staring blankly at a rack of maternity jeans. A young woman dressed in black with piercings stopped before me, staring first. "You shop at Kmart," she observed, more as a statement than a question. "Legit."

However, the woman at the airport did not want to talk. Instead, she stood next to me at the sink, leaning in so close that I could feel her heat on my cheek. I leaned back slightly, my hands still under the tap. "I just wanted to say thank you," she remarked. There was a pause before she said, "Thanks for ruining the country."

Then she turned around and vanished into a restroom stall, leaving me standing there like a high schooler who had just been hazed.

I considered tapping on her stall door. I am sorry, I imagined asking through the door. Could you perhaps be more specific? It's just that "you ruined the country" is an overly broad statement, considering that there are nearly limitless ways to ruin a country. Do you mean damaged the economy or the healthcare system? I am sure I have a number of retorts, but first I need to know what you mean. Instead, I dried my hands and left.

Obviously, not all of my conversations throughout the years had been nice. And that is fine. I grew up in a debate-rich environment, and I'd had numerous conversations with folks who disagreed with my political views. But, with just a few exceptions—such as the elderly man who had persistently followed me while I purchased underwear and bras at Farmers until my protection officer intervened—I was grateful to have them. I appreciated that I wasn't enclosed in a "head of state" bubble. I even scheduled additional time for each errand so that I might have these spontaneous talks.

However, this bathroom episode felt unusual. It was the woman's tone of voice, the fact that she had stood so near, and her seething, generic wrath that felt not just unpredictable but also out of place in the context. It reminded me of a time when a father asked me to photograph his daughter, a young woman in a wheelchair, inside a mall. I crouched down with the girl, smiling broadly and keeping one eye on Neve, who was waiting nearby. A woman approached the parent alone as he held up his phone to take a photo. The woman stayed there for a few moments before I looked over. When our gazes connected, she raised both middle fingers at me, her face a map of indistinguishable wrath, and walked away.

What was going on? Whatever it was, it was not limited to New Zealand. Something had been loosened over the world. Around the world, I heard reports of not only politicians, but even high-profile public servants, particularly those working on COVID, being followed and harassed in the streets. And sometimes worse. Shinzo Abe, Japan's prime minister—the quiet but serious man who had told me how sad he was when my cat died and who had helped finalize the CPTPP trade deal—was shot and killed by a member of the public who believed him to be affiliated with a church he blamed for his family's destitution.

There has always been those who disliked politicians. I knew that. But it seemed like something had shifted recently, as if people's inhibition had loosened. Perhaps it was the ideal storm, where the online world helped to reduce leaders to nothing more than "politicians," which was somehow distinct from being human, making all of us more vulnerable to assault. Or maybe my resilience, my capacity to get through a problem, was deteriorating. Perhaps it was both.

I had been running on adrenaline for so long. All those restless nights, all that cortisol, all that fight or flight exhausts a person. And it wasn't just how I felt inside. It appeared to be something I wore on the outside, too. People frequently told me I looked exhausted. Gaunt. More than one person advised I eat a beef pie. You make a good point. I couldn't eat when I was stressed, and I'm constantly stressed these days.

It's strange that everything was hitting at once. This time was relatively peaceful compared to the previous five years. Days returned to some consistency. But I couldn't enjoy them or relax into the relative serenity.

Perhaps I was conditioned to deal with crises. I knew the next challenge, whatever it was, was around the corner. And when it came, I'd need a full tank with plenty of reserves. And I wasn't sure I had it anymore.

It was time to express what had previously been a private notion.

CHAPTER 22

It was quiet when I had said the words, just the two of us in my office. The door was closed, and it was late enough in the evening that you couldn't hear the usual hum of movement in the office next door. Instead, it was Grant's groan that filled the silence.

I had just told Grant I was thinking about leaving. I was seated behind my desk, Grant facing me in a black leather chair, his hands resting on top of his head as he tried to stretch out his pained back. When I first said the words aloud, "I think I should leave," he squeezed his eyes shut as if trying to block out something he wished he hadn't heard. Eventually, he opened his eyes and took a deep breath.

"Well, you know what I am going to say." I remained silent. "Professionally," he said, "I want you to stay."

Grant, my friend, the person who'd been looking out for me since we first met in the Beehive cafeteria years ago, when he could see I was lost in Harry's office and I didn't know what came next. Who had brought me onto the ninth floor, and who'd ensured I'd ranked above him on the party list.

Now, as he looked at me from across my desk, he had the same expression on his face that he'd had almost six years earlier, when he'd walked into the caucus room after years of trying and failing to become leader, only to hear he'd lost again by one percent. It was a look that said, I'm so sorry, as if somehow he owed me something. It was as if after all these years of friendship and working together, my departure meant he had let me down.

After a long pause, he glanced down.

"But personally, as your friend," he continued. Then lifting his head up, he met my eye. "As your friend, I support you to go."

There were so few people I could talk to about my possible departure. If it ever came out that I was considering leaving, the decision would almost certainly be taken out of my hands. You can never doubt yourself as a leader, at least not publicly. To do so would imply you were no longer committed to the job. But if there was one other person in my inner circle who needed to know, it was my chief of staff, Raj.

I knew it wouldn't be a clinical discussion for Raj; the reason I loved working with him was he placed emphasis on both head and heart. But when we talked, it was almost as if he couldn't find his way to objectivity. Instead, for each point I made, he produced a counterpoint. Something that was useful in a political situation but pained me in this one.

"Whatever it is about the job you are struggling with, there will be a fix," he argued, adding, "Election year is a reason to stay, not leave—the team needs you." But I pushed back, listing the many reasons I believed the team would be better off if I left.

I even shared with Raj a consideration I hadn't shared with Grant. I said I thought I had become a flashpoint, a political lightning rod. One that might cause an electoral swing and unravel the work we'd done. If by stepping aside I could take the heat out of the politics, I explained, perhaps I could prevent a backlash that would undo all the progress we'd made—on race relations, on women's rights, and for the LGBTQ+ community.

I had nothing to back up my theory, and even the polling at the time had just a few points between us and our opposition. But it was a feeling I had, and as the words came out of my mouth, I felt even more sure about what I was saying. But Raj disagreed.

He was sitting where Grant had sat just days before, but unlike Grant he approached the conversation as if I might change my mind. "But you leaving won't fix that," he finished.

I looked at him silently. Right there, sitting just as we were now, we had spent countless hours over the last five years debating and discussing everything, from the tiniest details of our waste reduction policies and climate work, to the ordering of the cabinet agenda and the travel plans of ministers. Raj was no longer just a colleague; he was now one of my closest friends. I trusted his judgment implicitly. So, I knew that if I left him sitting in silence, he would understand exactly what I was saying.

Leaving might make our politics feel calmer, less polarized. And it might not. But I was beginning to believe that I'd rather leave and be wrong than stay and be right.

He shook his head. "I'm not saying there isn't an issue there. I just think you're the one who can take us through the next election. Who can make Labour's case." There was no denying there was more to do. The gap in our tax system, for one thing. Grant, David Parker, and I had kicked off work on an alternative to a capital gains tax—but maybe even that would be easier to implement without me?

"Labour doesn't need me to win," I told him. I believed that. We were polling about 34 percent, roughly three points shy of where we were when we were elected in 2017. For everything New Zealand had been through since—a pandemic, a volcano, floods, fires—this wasn't bad. But it did need to be better, and I believed it could be. With someone else as head of the party.

But this wasn't just a decision about winning, or even about whether I was some kind of flash point. It was also about whether I could do another four years with everything the job demanded. Whether I still had all the energy and enthusiasm, the curiosity and open mind required of a good leader. As prime minister, you have to be on high alert all the time. At any moment, you can find yourself managing a situation that requires total focus—making one decision after the next, operating on minimal sleep and under maximum pressure. You have to be your best. Was I still bringing my best to this role? And could I for four more years?

And so, I took in the feedback from Raj, someone I trusted completely, and for the first time I could remember, I dismissed it.

After all, Raj had already told me he was leaving.

There were many other things to focus my mind on over the coming weeks. We extended our support for Ukraine by deploying extra infantry training teams to train its personnel in the U.K. We rolled out a retail crime prevention fund to try to take on a surge in ram raids—cars driving into shops and robbing them. And at the Labour Party Conference, I laid out a significant expansion of Childcare Assistance subsidies that meant 54 percent of all New Zealand families with children would be eligible for support, and nearly every sole parent. We continued to make progress on climate and child poverty, and I traveled to APEC and the East Asia Summit, all while making plans to kick off the new year by announcing the election date.

But inside it was always there, that same thought: Should I go?

One night I lay in bed with Clarke in Auckland, trying to decide what to do.

"You don't want me to quit, do you?" I asked. These days, Neve had settled into a new day care, and she and Clarke traveled with me less often. Nearby my small black travel bag and briefcase were leaning against the wall, ready for me to sneak out in the morning and head back to Wellington for another week in Parliament.

"I want you to do what you feel comfortable with," Clarke said. We'd had this exact conversation before, and he'd said these words before, too.

"I want to know what you think."

"I think we'll be fine whatever you decide," Clarke said. I sighed in quiet frustration. I wanted some kind of reaction, something that might help tip the scales of my own thinking.

We lay there for a while. I stared at a rectangle of light cast from one of the windows. Outside were our unkempt gardens. It was getting close to the holidays, the one time we ever seemed to have a chance to do yard work and to think.

Clarke took a deep breath. "I just don't want them to feel like they've won," he said. I didn't need to ask whom he was talking about. He meant the ones who could never stick to policy, the ones who made it personal, the ones who labeled me a flake, stupid, or vapid or who went after my family. Those who thought a rumor was a weapon, and that physical threats just came with the job.

I knew what Clarke was saying. I didn't want "them" to win either. But hadn't I defeated them already, by being there in the first place and then by persisting? Every day, people demanded I prove myself, and I had. And I don't just mean through all the crises—a M.bovis outbreak, a terrorist attack, a volcanic eruption, a pandemic, and more. I hadn't become cynical. I hadn't resorted to cheap shots. I hadn't fundamentally changed who I was or what mattered to me.

I was finished proving myself. There was only one question I needed to answer now, and it wasn't one that would be posed by my critics. It was mine: Did I want to keep going?

Several months after I'd first broached the topic of stepping down with Grant, I stood in a hotel room, in front of a wardrobe, trying to decide what to wear. Since becoming prime minister, I'd made this decision, usually the first of the day, more than nineteen hundred times. Now here I was, choosing between the only two dresses I'd brought with me on this trip.

It was the start of a new political year. The Labour Party would, as usual, mark this new start with an "away" caucus, a retreat that would allow us to plan for the year ahead. This year, the retreat was in Napier, an important swing electorate. Clarke, Neve, and I had flown in the night before. We'd arrived late, eaten snacks for dinner, and tried to settle Neve into yet another hotel room.

I never stopped visiting schools when I became prime minister. In fact, it was one of the most consistent things I did as a politician. And when the opportunity arose, I would still go through the same exercise with students on leadership that I always had, asking them the same question: "What does a politician look like?"

I did this exercise dozens of times through the years. I would ask the students to tell me what they physically saw, and what they heard. The words that would come flying sometimes broke my heart: Selfish. Old. Untrustworthy. Liar. Bald.

It was never lost on me that there I was, a politician, standing in front of students and asking them to describe one, only to have them describe traits that I thought belonged to someone else. But that was my point. I was trying to explore our underlying assumptions. To show that sometimes we think that jobs or roles require you to have certain traits or ways of being, and maybe that was something we should challenge.

On one such school visit, this time on a marae, I put this same question to a group of young people, maybe fifteen or sixteen years old, sitting on the floor in front of me. "What does a politician look like?"

The first time, I noticed some differences. The word "woman" was used for starters. Not all traits were those of type A personalities either. I saw a young woman in the front slowly, tentatively raise her hand. I gestured to her, and she lowered her hand back to her lap. She sat forward a little bit as she offered me a word that in all these years no student ever had.

"Kind," she said. "I think politicians can be kind."

I smiled at her. "Yes," I said. "I think they can be kind, too."

Years earlier, I had counted myself out of politics, assuming that a politician who was kind, or who was sensitive, maybe even filled with self-doubt, was one destined to fail. The political leadership model, it seemed, was too rigid to be broken. And yet here I was now, prime minister, standing in front of a girl who was saying the very thing that once seemed impossible. Maybe that meant it would be different for her.

Maybe by the time this girl was my age, kindness in politics wouldn't be an anomaly; it would be the norm. Maybe we'll have many, many leaders who don't fit old assumptions. Maybe this girl will even be one of them. If she is, she might have doubts along the way; she might question herself, her ability to be there.

And if she does, here is what I would tell her. Here is what I would say to everyone who doesn't fit the old mold:

If you have impostor syndrome, or question yourself, channel that. It will help you. You will read more, seek out advice, and humble yourself to situations that require humility to be conquered. If you're anxious, and overthink everything, if you can imagine the worst-case scenario always, channel that too. It will mean you are ready when the most challenging days arrive. And if you are thin-skinned and sensitive, if criticism cuts you in two, that is not weakness; it's empathy. In fact, any traits you believe are your flaws will come to be your strengths. The things you thought would cripple you will in fact make you stronger, make you better. They will give you a different kind of power, and make you a leader that this world, with all its turmoil, might just need.

That is what I would tell her.

And I suppose in sharing my story, that's what I'm telling you.

Less than a week after that visit to Napier, I was back in Wellington, in the rear seat of a ministerial car. Clarke sat next to me, his arm leaning against the passenger window. We'd just dropped Neve off at day care. I pulled out my phone and opened the contact information for John Campbell, the reporter who'd interviewed me on a bright October day, years earlier, when I was heading to be sworn in to a job I'd never imagined having.

John didn't answer—busy reporting the news, I imagined—so I decided to leave him a voice memo.

Hey, John, I said. The car was rolling down Featherston Street. I'm just in the car and on the way to Government House to officially resign.

Back in Napier, when I'd left Neve and Clarke in the hotel room, I'd walked into a small, unadorned conference room to break the news to the cabinet. I was stepping down. Then I went to the larger, upstairs space, overlooking the sea, where caucus was assembled, and told them. Then, finally, I held a press conference, and I told the country.

Now I was heading to Government House, where a new Labour prime minister, Chris Hipkins, would be sworn in.

I wasn't done. I wasn't done trying to help people, to make the world a little brighter. I'd never be done with those goals. I just wasn't going to do it as prime minister anymore.

I had not been everyone's first image of a leader, including my own. I was a very ordinary person who found themselves in a set of extraordinary circumstances. But I had been a leader. And I had done it on my own terms.

In these final moments as prime minister, the car was passing Queens Wharf. I finished my message to John. Despite how I sound, I said, I'm leaving with nothing but happiness.

Yes, I realized. I was happy. Happiness is a lot of things. And I had found plenty of it in this unexpected job I'd had. But the happiness I felt now came from knowing simply that I had done my best. Whatever the challenge, whatever came at me, I had done my best. And that was enough.

I hung up the phone and looked forward, toward the road in front of us, toward the moments that I still couldn't imagine, toward everything that still lay ahead.

A new era was about to begin.

Printed in Dunstable, United Kingdom